THE 7 PRINCIPLES of HIGHLY ACCOUNTABLE ★★★★ MEN

mark r. laaser

BEACON HILL PRESS
OF KANSAS CITY

Copyright 2011 by Mark R. Laaser and
Beacon Hill Press of Kansas City

ISBN 978-0-8341-2742-5

Printed in the
United States of America

Cover Design: Brandon Hill
Interior Design: Sharon Page

Library of Congress Cataloging-in-Publication Data

Laaser, Mark R.
  The 7 principles of highly accountable men / Mark R. Laaser.
    p. cm.
  Includes bibliographical references.
  ISBN 978-0-8341-2742-5 (pbk.)
  1. Christian men—Religious life. 2. Responsibility. 3. Christian life. I. Title. II. Title: Seven principles of highly accountable men.
  BV4528.2.L33 2011
  248.8'42—dc23

2011024608

10 9 8 7 6 5 4 3 2 1

CONTENTS

Acknowledgments   5

Introduction   7

1. Principle One: Accountability Begins with Brokenness, Confession, and Repentance   11

2. Principle Two: Accountability Requires Your Being Able to Talk About Your Feelings and Needs   20

3. Principle Three: Accountability Always Requires a Group of Men or Women, Not Just One Person   45

4. Principle Four: Accountability Means You Must Get Rid of the Garbage in Your Life   58

5. Principle Five: Prepare When You Are Strong for a Time When You Will Be Weak   78

6. Principle Six: Accountability Means Building and Defending in Equal Measures   91

7. Principle Seven: To Change a Negative Behavior, You Must Do Whatever It Takes for As Long As It Takes   105

Conclusion—Accountability Is a Lifestyle   119

Notes   123

Resources   125

ACKNOWLEDGMENTS

No one really writes a book alone. There are those who have contributed ideas, those who have reviewed ideas and content, and those who support through encouragement and prayer. That has certainly been the case for me.

First and foremost is the person who has contributed, reviewed, encouraged, and prayed the most—my wife, Debbie. We have been married for thirty-eight years. During that time she has gone through the good times and the bad and never stopped being my number one friend, companion, and soul mate. She is often way ahead of me emotionally and spiritually. She has been the main way that God has demonstrated his grace to me. It has been our ministry together helping couples survive the crisis of infidelity that has shaped and formed many of the ideas in this book series. To Debbie, I can never say thank you enough.

A great deal of inspiration has come through my work with men who struggle with infidelity and sex addiction. Each and every one of the hundreds I have worked with has taught me something. There is a smaller number who really helped shape the material in this book. Anonymity issues prevent me from recognizing them more publicly.

Several men introduced me to certain concepts in these books. I am honored to say that they are colleagues and friends. Chris Charleton first pointed me to the powerful example of the story of Nehemiah and how it reveals to us a plan for accountability. Eli Machen is a superb teacher on many subjects, and his ideas on vision are what originally influenced me about it. More recently, Greg Miller has been helping me more fully understand the value of our needing a team of people to help us heal. To all of these men I say, "Thank you very much!"

To the wonderful family of people at Beacon Hill Press of Kansas City, thank you for your confidence, faith, and trust in me. Eric Bryant originally approached me about this series, and Bonnie Perry has nurtured it along.

And in all things to God be the glory. There are times for all Christian writers, I think, when they try to simply sit at the computer, quiet their spirits, and invite God to give them insight and inspiration. I pray that all readers of these books will open themselves to this quiet place and will allow God to speak to them directly through the imperfect words, thoughts, and ideas of this series. I could not put any book out there if I did not think that God was in charge of the process.

—Mark R. Laaser
January 2011

INTRODUCTION

Have you ever wanted to change something in your life? You may have wanted to start a new and healthy behavior or to stop an old and unhealthy one. Maybe you have wanted to start exercising or to stop watching so much TV. Or has it been more serious, such as wanting to start a deeper spiritual time of prayer and Bible study or to stop a destructive addiction? Have you been starting or stopping but frustrated because you have been unable to sustain the change? The apostle Paul puts it this way in Rom. 7:19, "For what I do is not the good I want to do; no, the evil I do not want to do—this I keep on doing."

I have had to start and stop many behaviors in my life. As a recovering addict, I have experienced many addictions I have needed to stop—sinful sex, nicotine, caffeine, and food. I have also needed to start healthy behaviors—exercising, eating healthy, maintaining my male friendships, and practicing spiritual disciplines. In this book I would like to share with you the seven principles of accountability I have learned that have continually helped me with those changes.

Change is a process and often takes longer than we think. For many of us it is a lifetime journey. To achieve true change, a person must be accountable to others to make that change. I would therefore like to share with you what true accountability is all about. Over the years I have seen many people struggle with addiction because they don't fully understand the foundation of accountability.

There are two sources of these seven principles. The first source comes from the wisdom found in most addiction recovery programs. In essence, whether these programs are secular or Christian, they have built their core structure on the twelve steps of Alcoholics Anonymous (AA). Here is a short history of AA. In 1935, Bill Wilson was on a business trip to Ohio. After years of struggle with alcoholism, he had finally found sobriety through a rather remarkable spiritual experience while hospitalized. Now, at a hotel in Ohio, he found it hard to pass by the hotel bar and not go in. So Bill W. (as he is known by millions) called every local pastor and priest until one finally told him to go talk to the town drunk, Dr. Bob Smith. Dr. Bob had not yet been able to stop his drinking. When they met one fateful night, Bill asked Bob to help him by simply listening to his struggles. Bill W. was not there to preach at him. He was there desperate and needy. As they talked through the night, the essence of what was to become the twelve steps was formed. That first AA meeting has led to thousands of meetings around the world and millions of lives saved from the ravages of alcoholism.[1]

Each in their own way, Bill W. and Dr. Bob, had been influenced by Christian principles. Those of us who have really strived to "work" the steps and who are Christian know that they are totally consistent with our theological understanding of who God is and what the Bible teaches. As you read and seek to digest what I have to teach you in this book, you will find the twelve steps are a strongly influential source.

The second source, which will really provide the structure of this book, is from two Old Testament sources. First, the book of Nehemiah, at least the first six chapters, contains the truths of the seven principles of highly accountable men. Second, the story of the exodus of the Jewish people out of the land of Egypt will illustrate the core essence of how people change.

As you read this, let me offer you several words of encouragement and instruction. Those of us who have tried to change a behavior and often failed are full of shame. Shame is a very biblical emotion and in a healthy way can remind us that we need God in our lives. Shame can also be a very deadly emotion when it becomes the feeling that we are bad and worthless persons, perhaps even that we are a mistake. When any of us experience difficulty in changing, we feel a confirmation that we will never get it right. Ultimately, shame leads many of us to believe that not even God can love us.

Nothing could be further from the truth. The Bible is clear. We are "fearfully and wonderfully made" (Ps. 139:14), God loves us so much that he sent his only Son to save us (John 3:16), and there is no sin that can separate us from the love of God (Rom. 8:39). In truth, you can change. The first part of accountability will be to find those around you who might remind you of God's truth. Let me be the first: "You are a wonderful child of God and change is possible."

It is my hope that this book will be a blessing to you.

1

PRINCIPLE ONE
ACCOUNTABILITY BEGINS WITH BROKENNESS, CONFESSION, AND REPENTANCE

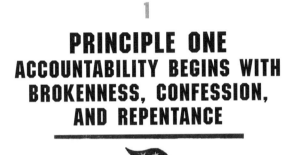

The Story of Nehemiah

In Jewish history God has at times become angry enough with Jewish disobedience that he has allowed the enemies of the Jews to have their way. Such was the case in the sixth century BC, and this time the Babylonian empire was the conquering enemy. The occupation strategy of the Babylonians was often to take captured people to Babylonian territory and cities in order to assimilate them into Babylonian culture. Sadly the ten northern tribes of Israel had succumbed to this strategy. Some of those assimilated peoples became the Samaritans with whom so much conflict was to develop with those faithful Jews of the two southern tribes. Later in our story we will see it is one of those Samaritans, Sanballat the Horonite, who is the main enemy of the rebuilding project Nehemiah undertakes.

Nehemiah was a descendant of the Jewish population that had been taken captive to Babylon in 587-586 BC. In 539 BC Cyrus the Persian gained control over all of Mesopotamia, and the Persian Empire was to rule this area until the time of Alexander the Great. Cyrus was a benevolent man and permitted the Jewish exiles to return to the city of Jerusalem. This return, however, was not well received by the exiles' neighbors, including the Samaritans, and any rebuilding project had continually been defeated. Nearly a century later, in Nehemiah's time, the Persian ruler was Artaxerxes I Macrocheir, who ruled between 465 BC and 424 BC. Nehemiah was not a descendant of the exiles who had returned to Jerusalem. Instead he was still in Persia and had continued to participate in Persian life and culture. Nehemiah was the personal cupbearer to King Artaxerxes. Because terrorism existed in those days, Nehemiah's job was to make sure no one was trying to poison the king. It was a somewhat dangerous job, but it did allow him to "hang out" with the most powerful man in the universe.

In 445 BC Nehemiah learned of the deplorable condition of the returned exiles in Jerusalem. It was probably because of his proximity to the power of the day that a delegation from Jerusalem, including Hanani, who Nehemiah claims as one of his brothers, came to see him. At that time he was in Susa, a citadel. They told Nehemiah that the wall of the city was broken down, the gates were burned, and the people were in distress. This is the sad and depressing opening of our story.

Brokenness

We know that Nehemiah is going to be a great leader and reformer. So as our story opens what would you expect a great leader to do when he hears the news of such destruction? Have you ever been to a leadership conference in one of our great churches such as Willow Creek Church? If so, what have you heard about how a leader would react? Would he not take charge and have an idea of what to do next? That might be a legitimate expectation, but that is not Nehemiah at this point. Nehemiah, himself, says, "When I heard these things, I sat down and wept. For some days I mourned and fasted and prayed before the God of heaven" (Neh. 1:4).

Nehemiah was sad and broken. There is nothing about this sadness in our stereotypes of what a leader should be like. On second thought, however, maybe there is. Remember that for about one hundred years every attempt to rebuild Jerusalem had failed. At this point, Ezra, who was so successful at religious reforms (see chaps. 8–10), was already in Jerusalem and had been for thirteen years. Many things about the condition of Jerusalem had improved, but a city without protection was a city vulnerable to constant attack and plunder. To not have a walled city with protection was a sign of considerable disgrace to the Jews of that time. Nehemiah had no reason to believe he could be more successful in any rebuilding effort. He had no experience in building. He was simply discouraged and sad and was so for days. Perhaps that is where true leadership begins. It doesn't start with a sense of personal strength. Rather, it begins with a sense of one's own limitations and a belief that he or she really needs God.

Those who are confident don't think they need to be accountable. They don't think they need any help. Perhaps they are overconfident and even self-centered. They won't ask for help. On the other hand, those who are broken know they need help. They also know that if they are going to do anything, including changing something, they will need to be accountable. Nehemiah needed to change something, one hundred years of frustration and despair in Jerusalem. Yet he had no idea at this point about how to do that.

✷ POINT TO PONDER

Accountability can only begin when we know that we need help and that we can't do it alone.

✷ QUESTIONS TO PONDER

- Have you ever heard news that caused you to feel overwhelmed with sadness?

- Have you ever been discouraged by some project or task?

- Have you ever tried to do or change something and failed miserably?

- How are you at asking for help?

- Do you ever allow yourself to feel sad and to express that sadness?

Confession

So being broken, Nehemiah starts where we all should start. He asks God for help and prays a prayer. The first part of the prayer is a prayer of confession. Nehemiah prays, "I confess the sins we Israelites, including myself and my father's house, have committed against you. We have acted very wickedly toward you. We have not obeyed the commands, decrees and laws you gave your servant Moses" (1:6-7). Nehemiah recognizes that sin has had something to do with the miserable condition of the Jews in Jerusalem. They had not trusted God and had not obeyed his commands. Nehemiah knew that the covenant relationship the Jews had with God required them to be obedient and that when they weren't, they were subject to God's punishment.

In the New Testament James tell us how important confession is: "Therefore confess your sins to each other and pray for each other so that you may be healed. The prayer of a righteous man is powerful and effective" (James 5:16). Confession is totally necessary when we first know we need help and we are humble and broken. When we think we don't need help, we often lie to others who ask us how we're doing and we say, "Fine." For most of us, most of the time, that is just not true.

✸ POINT TO PONDER

We can only be accountable and receive God's grace and help when we truly get honest with God and with others. This is what confession is all about.

✸ QUESTIONS TO PONDER

- Are there any behaviors in your life you are ashamed of and have not told anyone about?

- Is the behavior you want to change one you have never discussed with anyone or asked anyone for help with?

- Have you ever confessed a sin to someone such as your spouse, friends, or pastor/priest?

- If you have, what did it feel like to do so?

- Would you be willing to schedule a time to do so with someone you consider an important spiritual influence in your life?

Repentance

The next part of Nehemiah's prayer is talking to God about repentance. In Neh. 1:8-9 he "reminds" God of a promise that if the Jewish people will return to God and obey God's command-ments, God will return them to their home even if they are scat-tered to the farthest corner of the earth.

My favorite story of repentance is that of the prodigal son in Luke 15. Jesus is painting a picture of the powerful love of a father who continually waits for his son to return. In describing the degradation of a son who has wasted his dad's money in a foreign land, Jesus says that the son sunk so low he wound up feeding pigs. He is literally in the pigpen. The son even longs to eat the pods that pigs eat, but no one will even give him those. This image is quite powerful because, as you know, Jews don't eat pigs. To not even be able to eat what pigs eat is about as low as a Jew could sink. In the midst of that scene the son comes to his senses and realizes he should return to his father, and on the way he practices his confession. He is willing to even live as one of his father's servants. Don't we love the ending to this story in which Jesus tells us that even when the son is a long way off, his father rushes out to meet him.

This is quite the picture because to run out to meet his son, the father has to pick up his robes. To expose your feet and legs in this way was terribly against Jewish culture and a true sign of humility or degradation. In other words, the father humbles himself. Jesus is preparing the listener for the true character of God. When we humble ourselves, become willing to confess and repent, God will rush out to meet us. Later, Jesus will humble himself even to the point of death so that God's grace can be freely given to us.

In our story of Nehemiah an essential part of his humility and brokenness is his willingness to confess the sins of the Jewish people and to tell God they will be repentant. This sets up the rest of the story in which Nehemiah himself will return to the home of the Jews, Jerusalem.

Most of us are familiar with the concept of repentance. We often have opportunities in our church services for those who want to repent to come forward in addition to those who want to accept Christ for the first time. In my experience, what we are not so good at in the church is having opportunities to confess.

Understand that our Roman Catholic brothers and sisters have considered confession an act of reconciliation, and as such it is a sacrament. There are regular and frequent opportunities for them to go to a priest and unburden themselves of their sins. Perhaps it is time, in my opinion, for us Protestants to come up with regular ways in which we can confess our sins to a pastor or church leader. I'm not talking about some printed confession in the Sunday bulletin. No, face-to-face confession, I believe, is much more important.

The twelve-step program of Alcoholics Anonymous has built confession into the process of getting sober. In the fourth step, AA asks the addict to make a "searching and fearless moral inventory."[2] Step five then asks the addict to directly confess that inventory to someone else.[3] I have always believed that the person to whom I need to confess must be a person I consider a spiritual authority. That is the only way I will feel that he or she has the power to remind me of God's grace.

Many of you may be carrying around guilt and shame from behaviors you have never told anyone about. The weight of that guilt and shame has kept you bogged down in an endless dark hole. Change is often hard if not impossible when we carry the weight of our sins around with us. You have probably thought that if anyone knew these behaviors, he or she would reject you and leave you. This might be especially true of your spouse. I have always found that usually the opposite happens. When a person gets truly humble and honest, other people begin to be "Jesus with skin on."

In my experience we learn a lot about confession and a willingness to ask for help in our families. What was your life like in your family and in the culture around you? Did your parents, caregivers, teachers, pastors, or friends ever say, "I'm sorry? I made a mistake. It was my fault. Can you please forgive me?" If this kind of modeling was not a part of your life, you learned to deny your sins, minimize them, or blame others for why bad things happen.

✹ POINT TO PONDER

Accountability demands us to be humble, broken, and willing to ask for help, confess, and repent.

✹ QUESTIONS TO PONDER

- Have you ever felt completely ashamed of a behavior you haven't been able to change?

- Do you recognize that this behavior might be the result or consequence of being disobedient to God?

- Have you ever realized you need to return to God's commandments?

- Has your shame prevented you from wanting to talk to anybody about it?

- Has your shame kept you stuck in a dark place and immobilized you?

- Try to imagine the image of God rushing out to meet you if you would decide to return to him?

2

PRINCIPLE TWO
ACCOUNTABILITY REQUIRES YOUR BEING ABLE TO TALK ABOUT YOUR FEELINGS AND NEEDS

Feelings

The foundation of change has been laid. Nehemiah is humble and broken. He has confessed the sins of the Jewish people and he has told God that the people would be repentant and willing to return to God's ways. And Nehemiah is still sad.

This must have been a new experience for Nehemiah because in Neh. 2:1 he says he has "not been sad in [the king's] presence before." Nehemiah is going about his normal job and has prepared wine for the king, and his sadness must have been obvious, because in verse 2 the king asks him why his face is so sad. The king has noticed that Nehemiah is not physically sick, and he therefore makes a diagnosis when he says, "This can be nothing but sadness of heart" (v. 2).

In verse 3 Nehemiah doesn't deny he is sad or say something such as, "No, no, I'm really fine." Instead he says, "Why should my face not look sad when the city where my fathers are buried lies in ruins, and its gates have been destroyed by fire?" Doesn't it sound as though Nehemiah is not only sad but also a little angry?

How recently has someone asked you, "How are you?" And what have you said? If you're like most people, you probably said something to the effect that you are fine or good or okay. It is not unusual to be less than honest. When we ask someone how he or she is, we ordinarily don't expect an honest response. It is simply a polite greeting. And maybe sometimes you really are experiencing some difficult feelings. Since you are not in the habit of sharing, who then do you talk to?

So we really don't expect to get honest about our feelings in polite conversation. Yet at any one time we experience a variety of feelings. The question is, what do we normally do with those feelings? And why is this important? There is one main reason. When we don't share our feelings with those we love and those we want to be in relationship with, it keeps us isolated and even distant. This isolation creates loneliness, a feeling that most of us really don't like talking about. Many of us may not even realize that we are lonely. Loneliness and isolation will leave us without the strength and companionship of others. The community of others is what we will really need if we want to make changes. The bottom line is, how can we be accountable to anyone or any group if we don't know how to share our feelings?

Suppose that you have been trying to make some kind of change and that you are really frustrated with it, angry with yourself, anxious, and/or depressed. You might even feel hopeless or despairing. That is a difficult place to be by yourself. Perhaps, however, you have absolutely no practice in talking about feelings. Perhaps, also, you have inner beliefs that you must be strong and that only weak people have such "difficult" feelings. Sometimes our Christian beliefs are such that we think it is a sign of a lack of faith to share our "negative" feelings.

In my family, for example, I know there were lots of feelings. My dad was a pastor, and my mom was a pastor's wife. Both were raised during the Great Depression and then came into their adult years during World War II. These two "Greatest Generation" people had learned to survive a lot of difficult times. My dad left for Europe and got on a ship on his twenty-first birthday. My mom, a nurse at the time, worked, waited, wrote letters, and kept her feelings inside. Those times were tough, and it was necessary to be patient and strong, even courageous in the face of many hardships. That was a strength. What, however, did they learn to do with all of their feelings? I know they were both people of profound faith. They somehow believed that God would provide and that he was in charge. I certainly admire them for all of that.

Then, happy day of days, the men came home, and like thousands of other couples, they got married and proceeded to begin their lives together, including creating the baby boom generation. So in 1950 I came along. Today I know that the stresses of ministry for both of them were profound, and I'm fairly sure that neither one of them at that point knew how to share any feelings about it with each other. My dad worked and worked, and my mom continued to keep things to herself. My dad had many other ways of coping—and that is his story and not really mine to tell. Suffice it to say that there were some painful and sinful behaviors he got into. My mom knew about all of it because she told me later, but at the time you simply didn't talk about those things. You pressed on, and ministry was the ultimate determiner of what was important. My parents' belief was that you must put on a positive appearance. You wouldn't want to set a bad example of what faith was all about.

So what did this mean for me? Well, I learned at all costs to also put on a good appearance. I was the proverbial preacher's kid and expected to be a good example. If I ever began to have a feeling about anything, Scripture would always be quoted and some positive spin given. My dad accepted a new church during my high school years, and we moved during the summer between my junior and senior years. I was devastated and lonely, and a very real depression set it. My dad's favorite scripture at this kind of time was Rom. 8:28, and he assured me that "in all things God works for the good." He also said that I was getting the opportunity to make new friends and that I was developing social skills that would help me later in my life. My mother, the nurse, somehow got her hands on one of the early antidepressants, a drug she called her "sunshine" medicine, and she proceeded to give me a dose every morning. All I knew was that I really felt much better. Eventually I did make new friends, including the girl who would later become my wife.

In some ways my parents' words and actions were right. But what I also learned was that when you get into tough times, you simply cope by somehow medicating yourself to keep up a good appearance. Like my dad, I learned to work hard, quote Scripture, and look for other "distractions," including, in my case, pornography. Like my mother, I learned that there is always some chemical perhaps as simple as caffeine to take away my feelings.

Needless to say I brought this coping strategy into my marriage. So was I prepared for the intimacy God intends for a man and woman? Of course not, and since I really didn't know how to connect with another person, I was lonely. There was a distance between Debbie and me, but I wouldn't have known how to recognize it and talk about it. How could I be lonely when there were so many things to be thankful for, such as healthy children, a faithful wife, and good work to pursue? So I kept to myself, isolated and alone, and turned to my old coping strategies to survive. All of this continued to drive a wedge between Debbie and me, and even though I had countless "friends," none of them really knew what was going on inside of me.

I had a double life. There was my public life of ministry and my private life of coping. Everyone knew the first, and no one knew the second. I was accountable to no one, but my life needed to change. I remember so clearly how one of my first counselors challenged me to "get in touch" with my feelings. The key to that confrontation was that he and a group of men around me in a counseling group provided a safe setting for me to take my first baby steps in getting honest. When I did learn how to do that, my life and my marriage began to change.

● POINT TO PONDER

Accountability will proceed only when you know how to talk about your feelings.

● QUESTIONS TO PONDER

- How were feelings modeled in your family? Did you talk about them? Were you ever asked about them? What example did your parents give you?

- It's not only our families that provide this modeling. What did you learn about feelings at school, at church, or with your friends?

- How do you deal with feelings today? Do you ever feel lonely, angry, anxious, afraid, or sad? What happens with those feelings?

- Do you have anyone to talk to at all about feelings? If you are married, do you share your feelings with your spouse?

There is another reason for not being able to share feelings very well, and it is a difficult subject to talk about. In our story of Nehemiah he was a member of the Jewish remnant in Persia. The life of his people must have been very hard, a life filled with pain and suffering. When a person has experienced hardship or trauma, he or she sometimes has difficulty even talking about it, much less feeling the pain itself.

In my work with men and with couples, many of the people I counsel have experienced emotional, physical, or sexual pain in their lives. One of the young men I currently work with, for example, was abused by a camp counselor when he was fifteen. He was so ashamed of the experience that he didn't feel he could talk about any of it until only recently. Throughout high school and college he kept everything to himself, and it affected all of his relationships. He has never been able to get close to anybody because of the way he has shut down his feelings. He tells me he always believed that if he shared his feelings, they would get worse or other people would reject him as being somehow damaged. He feels certain he can't talk about this in church, since he was raised to believe he should be strong enough to get over it. Over the years he has developed a number of coping behaviors and abused various substances to deal with his pain. What brought him to me was that he wanted to change those behaviors and had not been able to. He will need the support in accountability of other men to do so.

This young man's situation is more common than many would admit. The pain of the past, however, doesn't always have to be as dramatic as being sexually abused or growing up in an alcoholic home. There are many situations in life—even some we might think are quite minor—that can affect our ability to express our feelings. One of the hot topics in our school systems at this time is bullying. Many kids are being emotionally shamed or frightened, not to mention physically harmed. This problem is as old as recorded history. There have always been those who want to torment others. Perhaps in some way you were teased, taunted, or threatened, even to the point of physical harm.

Something as accidental as birth order can cause pain in childhood. My wife and I are working with a couple in which the wife was the youngest of five children and the only girl. She was teased mercilessly by her brothers. Her father paid attention only to the boys and their athletic events and only took them hunting and fishing. The daughter experienced the pain of feeling she was unimportant. She coped by trying to be masculine in many ways that, now that she is married, completely alienate her husband.

This woman experienced a kind of pain that many of us do. She was abandoned, not literally, but emotionally. She never felt she fit in or belonged. When she was young, if she ever had feelings, the message from all the males in her family was, "Oh, you're just a girl." So she learned to suppress her feelings and hasn't really talked about them since. She would like to change, but who is she accountable to?

There are hundreds of ways we can be invaded or abandoned that create emotional pain. If we're unable to talk about this pain, it can be very isolating. In the story of King David and his family, one of his daughters, Tamar, was sexually abused by her brother Amnon. Later, Tamar's brother Absalom says to his sister, "Has that Amnon, your brother, been with you? Be quiet now, my sister; he is your brother. Don't take this thing to heart" (2 Sam. 13:20). The Bible then tells us that under this advice, Tamar lived in her brother's house a "desolate" woman. Desolation is often the price for quietness.

Often, like Tamar, we are quieted or even shamed for our feelings for spiritual reasons. I work with many men who have been sexually unfaithful to their wives in many different ways. Many of them who tried to take their feelings to their pastor or church leaders were ostracized. Their stories are, in my opinion, examples of the church "shooting its wounded." One of my colleagues was a pastor at a very large evangelical church. Unfortunately he sinned by having sex with another staff member. He was automatically fired and told to never attend that church again. He went from having his entire community centered at this church to being an outcast. Instead of working for his healing, the church treated him like a leper. Fortunately, he was able to find a therapist and group that encouraged him to talk about his feelings, including how the church had treated him. In doing that he became accountable and did begin his process of healing. He has been completely free of any sexually sinful behavior for over five years. He still, however, has to deal with the pain of how the church treated him.

● POINT TO PONDER

Pain from the past may have taught us not to share our feelings and, thus, to be very lonely.

● QUESTIONS TO PONDER

- Do you have memories of pain from your past?

- Have you been quiet about this for so long that you don't even realize it was painful?

- Have you ever tried to talk about your feelings to someone and had that person not listen or even blame or shame you for those feelings?

- Do you carry any spiritual pain from the past based on the teachings or the judgment of the church or its leaders?

- Would you be willing to talk to someone if you could find someone who is safe?

Needs

After Nehemiah expresses his feelings to King Artaxerxes, the king simply says to him, "What is it you want?" (Neh. 2:4). The king has heard his feelings, and because Nehemiah has been honest, the king asks him what he needs. You see, a person might not even know you need anything unless you can first get honest about your needs. Nehemiah is going to be honest and state his needs, but being careful, he starts by saying, "If it pleases the king" (v. 5). Often we are afraid that if we state our needs, someone might take offense. We wouldn't want to do that because someone might not be "pleased" with us.

We even take this attitude to God. For example, how many times have you used the word "just" in your prayers? Your prayers may start with the word "just": "Lord, I *just* pray that . . ." Jesus, however, instructs us to be bold when he says, "If you believe, you will receive *whatever* you ask for in prayer" (Matt. 21:22, emphasis added). We might as well ask for what we need because Jesus also says, "Your Father knows what you need before you ask him" (6:8). And we do need to ask even though God knows. Remember that whenever we ask God for anything, it should not be based on selfish desires but on our ongoing submission to his will for our lives.

So Nehemiah does ask for what he really needs. He wants to go back to the city of his fathers and "rebuild it" (Neh. 2:5). Strangely enough, the king tells him he can do it, since the king is, in fact, "pleased" by the request (v. 6). Empowered, Nehemiah also asks for some wood and some letters of safe passage (vv. 7-8).

This whole story would not have unfolded if Nehemiah had not truly taken a risk and asked for what he needed. One of the keys to this positive outcome is that he knew, at this point, what he really did need. He had a large need, to go home, and smaller needs for building materials and safe passage.

What do you need? If you are going to be accountable, you will have to know your needs. As you start thinking about them, don't be too "large" in your thinking. I'll talk about larger needs below. As I'm writing this, I need a break. It is dinner time and I need food. It is a rainy Sunday and I need a nap. Last night, Saturday, I told my wife I needed to play, so we went out to the mall and saw a movie. This morning she told me she needed me to go to the store and get some things for dinner. Do you get the idea? These are everyday needs, and we have lots of them.

Notice that not only do I have needs, but I also may need to ask for help to get them met. How are you at asking for help? Several years ago, I fell on some ice and cracked two of my ribs. Since I've had cracked ribs before, I knew there was nothing dramatic that could be done to speed their healing. Ibuprofen became my friend. The next morning I was supposed to give a speech to a large group of men at a nearby church, a Saturday morning men's prayer breakfast. I could barely get out of bed, and getting dressed was painful. I certainly couldn't bend down. When I did get to the church, I saw one of my friends in the lobby. I went up to him and simply asked, "Would you tie my shoes?" On the one hand, that is rather embarrassing. On the other, I was grateful he was a good friend, and he simply bent down and tied them. I might have tripped again if I hadn't asked someone for help with my needs.

If you are reading this book because you need to change something, have you become frustrated trying to bring that change about? Have you ever asked for help from anyone who might know how to help you? When alcoholics go to their first AA meeting, they will eventually admit that they are powerless over trying to stop drinking. At that point, they need the help of the group members. That may mean simply saying, "I need you to call me tomorrow and make sure I'm not drinking." It might also mean saying, "I need you to go out for coffee with me tomorrow so that I can have friendship and perhaps distract myself from my lustful thoughts." Ultimately, it might be a simple request: "I need you to pray for me."

In the previous section on feelings, I encouraged you to think about what you learned in your youth about feelings and about expressing them. Likewise, when it comes to needs, what did you learn about having those met when you were growing up? Some of us learn to simply take care of ourselves because no one was actually there. One of my friends grew up in a family in which his father constantly drank and his mother was emotionally broken and frequently wound up in the hospital. Even by age five he learned to feed himself, go to bed, and get up for school. When a younger sister and brother came along, he also learned how to care for them. From an early age he was an independent person, really much like an adult. Today, he has a hard time even believing he has needs that anyone could actually help him with.

The word "need" is often used when we really mean the word "should." In the men's groups I lead, I always have them check in with how they are feeling and what they need. I supply many of them with a chart of various feelings so that they can pick several. They will do this until they get more familiar recognizing them. As for needs, it is common for many of them to say, "I need to pray more," or "I need to make more calls to the men in the group." These are not "needs"; they are "shoulds."

✸ POINT TO PONDER

Expressing a need is really asking for help.

✸ QUESTIONS TO PONDER

- As you think about your upbringing, what did you learn about having needs?

- Have you ever asked anyone, including a spouse, to help you with a need?

- Are you often frustrated that no one ever seems to just offer to help you?

- As you read this page, can you identify at least one actual need you have, however small?

Large Needs

We all have rather large and universal needs. My wife and I call those the seven desires of the heart and have written a book about them by the same name.[4] Years ago we asked ourselves what needs God created inside all of us. We knew that God created "male and female" in "his own image" (Gen. 1:27). Since men and women are made in God's image, we felt they must have many things in common. We were tired of the teaching that men are from Mars and women are from Venus.[5] We knew that men and women learn many stereotypical social differences that become conditioned into them. But we were tired of trying to figure out "life on another planet" and decided to understand those ways men and women are both from earth. If we are from "different planets," we will feel we are strangers to each other, but if we are from earth and mutually created by God, then perhaps we could be companions.

So believing that men and women have the same universal needs, Debbie and I also felt that many of us don't always get those needs met as we grow up and that we learn to cope with that lack of fulfillment. For some, those ways of coping become extremely unhealthy behaviors and even addictions. I am writing this book for those of you who want to change those unhealthy behaviors. If you are going to be accountable to do so, you should know what the big needs or desires are.

As I list and describe them, try to think about your own life. Ask yourself how well you did about getting them met in childhood and later in your life. If you find that you didn't get them met, ask yourself how you learned to cope with that.

First is the desire to be *heard and understood.* We all need others to listen to us and to try and understand who we are or what we are saying. We need to be known. In the language of biblical Hebrew the word *yada* means "to know" and is used to describe how we know God and how we know each other. Don't you recognize how you have wanted God to know you and how you have wanted to know God? Don't you want God to hear you and understand your needs? When we don't feel we are heard, we can get loud, repetitive, unreasonable, or even belligerent. If we feel we are not being heard, we can shut down and not even try talking or we can search for others who will listen. Countless affairs have been started when one spouse finds another person who, at least on the front end of the relationship, is willing to listen.

Second is the desire to be *affirmed.* This is simply our need to have others tell us we did a good job. Affirmation is about our behavior. We love others to tell us we are appreciated. Hearing a thank-you from someone is an example of affirmation. Growing up many of us didn't get affirmed very much, if at all. Worse, some of us got criticized instead. When either of these situations is true, we will be starved for affirmation. We might do anything to get it, often working ourselves to death or conforming our behavior to what we think others will like. If we think we have to state a need for someone to affirm us, we believe that any resulting affirmation isn't really sincere. We reason that the person wouldn't have affirmed us if we didn't ask and so he or she doesn't really mean it.

Affirmation can also take the form of encouragement. This means others will tell us we can succeed or do something we might not think we can. Accountability, as we will see in a later principle, can often mean that others will "hold us accountable" to succeed, to help us believe we can change even when we think we can't.

Third is the desire to be *blessed*. Blessing is not about behavior. Affirmations are about behaviors. Blessing is about who we are. It happens when others tell us we are good people, they are glad we are who we are, and they are proud of us. When we are young, blessing is the job of our parents. Can you recognize that even today you long to hear from one or both of your parents that they are proud of you and that they are simply glad you are who you are? I consider it one of my main jobs in life to tell my kids regularly that I am proud of them and that they have become great and good people. This is true even though they are now adults. We can never get enough blessing.

If we don't feel that we ever get a blessing, we may feel shame. Shame tells us we are not good people, we will never get it right, and we can never succeed. Shame also tells us about relationships—that no one will really like us or that if anyone really knew us, he or she would hate us or leave us. Shame is the roadblock that tells many people they simply can't make the changes they should make.

Often when I work with men and with couples, I go out of my way to tell them that despite any behavior they have done, they are still great and good people and they are capable of doing better. In my role as pastor, I often remind them that God loves them and that just as he told his only Son, Jesus, God is "well pleased" with them (see Matt. 17:5). This is true because God forgives any and all sins. Accountability often means that others in our accountability network will remind us that we are good and capable of doing better. This is one of the great dynamics about any twelve-step or support group. We can go and confess all of our ugliest behavior, and people there will tell us they are glad we have come. We will get hugs and always be invited back.

Sometimes, we think the only way to get a blessing is to accomplish or achieve something. If we make a certain amount of money, live in a certain house, drive a great car, get the promotion, or earn the degree, then we will be blessed. That is a mistake in our thinking. It is confusing our need to be affirmed with our need to be blessed. No amount of accomplishment can bring us the blessing we all need.

Fourth is the desire to be *safe*. This is simply the need we have to be free of anxiety. We have anxiety about many things, such as our health, our financial well-being, our spiritual condition and the promise of eternal life, and our relationships. Anxiety is a very large feeling that we desire or need to be free of. For some of us, anxiety has been a lifetime issue. It can become debilitating and even lead people to take medication or seek professional counseling. Many studies have shown that anxiety is really a problem for those who grew up in unsafe situations at home or at school. Brain research confirms that when we are young and grow up in unsafe surroundings, the brain even develops in certain defensive ways. That is also true for those who have served during wartime and experienced the dangers of combat. For those of you for whom this is true, anxiety may have literally been conditioned into you and be an ongoing problem.

Since anxiety is so large, we might unconsciously "dumb it down" to thinking of it as a fear. One simple definition is that anxiety is about large life issues and that fear is about much smaller ones. Anxiety is usually very general, and fear is very specific. I have worked with a man, for example, who is greatly afraid that he has committed the unpardonable sin. He studies scriptures and consults various pastors with no relief. His anxiety is that he will not be going to heaven. That is large. I have another man who worries about his weight. He obsesses about what he eats and goes to the health club every day. He has a fear that if he gets too heavy, he will suffer very negative health consequences. This is very specific. Debbie and I are working with a couple in which the man had an affair over ten years ago. The wife continues to check his phone records and all bills and demands he call her five to six times a day so that she can be sure he is not involved with someone else. This wife's large anxiety is about being all alone, and she has "translated" this anxiety into daily fears about what her husband is doing.

It is often the task of our accountability group to remind us of what is true. For me, I have a large anxiety about well-being, which I dumb down to obsessing about whether the grass is mowed, the leaves are raked, or the snow is shoveled (depending on the season). My accountability group reminds me of the truth that God is in control of all our lives and that long grass, a few leaves, or a little snow never killed anyone. My group wouldn't know any of this if I hadn't been honest about my feelings and, in this case, my need to be safe.

Anxiety and the desire to be safe are the reasons people lie. Perhaps the largest anxiety of all is the anxiety of being all alone. A part of that anxiety is the belief that "if you really knew me, you would reject me and leave me." So we craft lies about what we've done and haven't done, what we've thought and haven't thought, and who we are and aren't. We want people to like us, to not be angry with us, and to remain in our lives. Have you ever lied to someone to manipulate that person's opinion of you?

Accountability groups and relationships will remind us of many truths. One of them is that God loves us no matter what we've done or who we've become. An accountability group reminds us we are liked, even with all of our sinful behaviors. Finally, an accountability group reminds us that we need to trust, take risks, and surrender control of how others think about us. In short, accountability encourages us to tell the truth.

Fifth is the desire to be *touched*. God has put two forms of this desire into our brains, both men and women. Since God instructs us in Genesis to "be fruitful, and multiply" (1:28, KJV), he has given all of us a desire to be touched sexually. That is very natural and we should never be ashamed if attractive people produce in us feelings of sexuality. That is our desire. What we decide to do with that desire is our choice, and God does command us to be "fruitful" only with our spouse.

The other form of this desire for touch that God has put into our brain is nonsexual. When we touch skin to skin, there is a very powerful chemical in the brain that gets released called oxytocin. This neurochemical gives us the feeling of well-being. If babies don't get touched enough, they will have a condition called "failure to thrive," and in extreme cases of deprivation, they can die. Adults, also, can suffer from touch deprivation.

The problem for some of us is that we confuse the need for sexual touch with the need for nonsexual touch. When this confusion takes place, an amount of energy gets added to the sexual drive. For some, a preoccupation with sex becomes the problem that we refer to as sexual addiction. For most, however, there is the idea that the only way they will ever get touched is by being sexual. All touch is either a prelude to being sexual or the result of sexual activity. We work with many couples who suffer from this confusion. They wind up afraid to hold hands because they fear it is about sex.

We recommend that everything about touch be intentional. If we simply want to hug, kiss, hold hands with a spouse, or even put our hand on someone else's shoulder, we believe we should ask. For those couples who are really confused about sex, we recommend that one person say to the other such statements as, "I want to give you a hug, and it is not at all about sex."

Nonsexual human touch is often a vital part of community and of encouragement. It gives us a sense of security and, as noted above, well-being. As such, it is essential to making changes. It is very hard, however, to allow it to happen and even worse to ask for it. I celebrate when one of the men in one of my groups gets up enough courage to ask for a hug.

Sixth is the desire to be *chosen.* All of us want to be wanted. Back in our younger days we longed to be picked for the team, to sit at the right lunch table, and to have a best friend. When we grow up, God has designed us in such a way that we long to be the only person in another person's life. We want to be chosen. It is the emotional and spiritual longing that creates monogamy and the intimate connection of one-flesh union. It is the force that drives us to one person. God knows that when we are intimately connected to one person in marriage, a spiritual bond is created that allows us to be faithful.

My favorite example of choosing occurs in the movie *Forrest Gump*. Forrest, as played by Tom Hanks, is mentally challenged and the target of jokes and bullying. The day he gets on the school bus for the first time, no one wants to sit with him. The children are cruel and go out of their way to keep him from sitting down. As he stands at the back of the bus with nowhere to sit, a young girl, Jenny, says, "You can sit here if you want." Forrest comes to love that girl for the rest of his life. He was chosen, an experience never to be forgotten.

Can you remember times when you felt chosen or not chosen? It can be a painful experience. Many of us go to great lengths to be chosen. We wear clothes the advertisers tell us to wear, drive cars that signal we have arrived, live in houses beyond our means, and alter our behavior to make us more "choosable." Plastic surgery is the fastest growing medical specialty because so many of us think we must look a certain way to be chosen.

What is so great about support groups for various problems, such as addictions, is that you don't have to succeed at anything to be chosen for them. Instead, you need to have failed at something. You may think that no one likes you, but at support group meetings you will have instant friends.

I have heard many men say that if they look at a little pornography or sneak a second look at an attractive woman, it's no big deal. To a wife, who wants to be chosen as the only one, it is a big deal. In the next book in this series I will deal with how we can avoid these temptations. To the men reading this now, understand that your wife or girlfriend has wondered about being chosen since she was a little girl. Why would you want to crush that spirit?

One of the great things I love about the stories of Jesus is that he often chose to be with people almost everyone considered unacceptable—the lepers, the invalids, the Samaritans, the sexual sinners, and the tax collectors. Moreover, Jesus chose us by dying for us.

Seventh and last is the desire to be *included*. This sounds much like the desire to be chosen, but while being chosen is the desire to be picked by one person, being included is the desire to belong to a larger group. The easiest way to understand the desire to be included is to think back to times when you felt you didn't belong. Have you ever felt left out of something? Perhaps it was the in-group of friends at school, the athletic team, a club or fraternity, or a job at a large company. When you think about belonging, haven't you really wanted to be part of a truly spiritual community, a church where God is glorified and people are safe and honest?

The benefits of community are endless. Studies have shown us that when we feel a part of community, we feel safe and supported. The health benefits are remarkable. In one study, it was shown that people who frequently attend church visit the doctor less because they have a lower incidence of disease.[6] Depression lifts when we are part of community. Conversely, loneliness has consistently been shown to contribute to all kinds of mental and physical health problems. God has designed us to belong. He calls us into families and into the family of God.

I've always been interested in language. One prefix that has always fascinated me is the prefix "dis." It means "to cut off."

When we add it to another word, it means "to cut off" from what that word signifies. So for example, we can be "disillusioned," which means we are "cut off from our vision." We can be disinherited, which means we can be "cut off from our inheritance." Concerning the desire to be included, we can certainly feel disconnected, which means we have been "cut off from our connection" to the community of God and others.

When you have felt disconnected and you long to belong, what have you done? The term "fit in" comes to mind. What have you done to "fit in"? We all, at times, seek to conform so that we will be accepted into various groups. We wear certain clothes, practice acceptable behaviors, and espouse acceptable beliefs. This is not always a bad thing. It is, however, unhealthy when we are doing something only to conform or to fit in. This happens when we go against our beliefs to avoid alienating others.

I think we do this frequently at church. We shine ourselves up and put smiles on our faces because we believe that God only loves happy people. Someone asks us at church how we're feeling and we respond by saying, "I'm fine." This often is a lie. We are not fine and might be depressed, sad, anxious, angry, or discouraged (that is, "cut off from our true heart"). We avoid saying something because we want to conform. Everyone else is smiling.

Paul tells us clearly in Rom. 12:2 that we should not conform to the ways of the world but that we should "be transformed by the renewing of [our] mind." I think of how much we conform today to the massive amounts of sexual immorality present in the world. We are so eager to be tolerant that we forget our God-given sense of what is right and wrong. We look past the sins of a president who has sexually abused an intern in the Oval Office. We watch TV shows and movies that are clearly immoral. We don't speak up when situations sexually offend us. Even our youth pastors are guilty of not teaching young people how to dress appropriately. We desperately want to belong, but sometimes at what cost?

Accountability does demand that we belong to groups of people who share our passion for change. Our community must consist of those who share our biblically centered beliefs. That is a truly safe community.

One final thought, the most important communities are the smallest: the community of a marriage, a family, a friendship.

❂ POINT TO PONDER

True change and healing will mean finding healthy ways to get the desires of our heart met in safe communities of accountability.

❂ QUESTIONS TO PONDER

- As you read about the seven desires, how well do you think you did receiving them when you were growing up?

- Are you aware of how you try to get each of the desires met? Another way of looking at this is how do you cope when you don't feel heard, affirmed, blessed, safe, touched, chosen, or included?

- Have you ever been able to tell someone else that you need one of these desires? For example, have you ever asked someone to simply listen, affirm you, or give you a hug?

- What feelings do you have when you believe that someone else hasn't met one of your desires?

- If one of those feelings is resentment, how do you deal with that?

- How are you at serving the desires of those you love, such as your spouse, your children, or a best friend?

Principle two of accountability will take a lot of practice. Some of the people I work with actually keep a piece of paper with various feelings written on it in their wallet or purse. They may practice by simply looking at it during the day and asking themselves what they are feeling at that moment. One of my friends keeps a small notebook with him, and every time he has a feeling or need he writes it down. At the end of the day he reads it to himself and often will share it with his wife or a friend.

Some people attend groups where participants are regularly asked to check in with their feelings and needs. Some of the couples we work with actually schedule a regular time each day when they state their feelings and needs to each other. If you would like to do that, remember that just because you state a need to someone it doesn't always mean he or she will meet that need. The ability to recognize and state a need is often a major victory.

Remember that accountability groups will include those people who model to you how to state feelings and needs. Accountability groups usually contain people who are further down the road and have had more practice than you. Being able to state your feelings and needs can be contagious.

Finally, realize that God is ultimately the one who truly knows your feelings and needs. Most importantly, he is the one who listens to you, affirms you, blesses you, keeps you safe, touches you through other people, chooses you, and includes you in his kingdom. Psalm 37:4 puts it this way, "Delight yourself in the LORD and he will give you the desires of your heart."

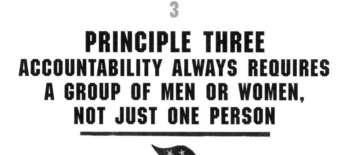

3

PRINCIPLE THREE
ACCOUNTABILITY ALWAYS REQUIRES A GROUP OF MEN OR WOMEN, NOT JUST ONE PERSON

A s the story of Nehemiah continues, King Artaxerxes is gracious and grants Nehemiah's request to go to Jerusalem. He gives Nehemiah the materials he needs and the letters of safe passage he asked for. At this point, Nehemiah is about to embark on this long journey by himself. Although he has not asked for any other help, the king is very wise and knows there is no way that Nehemiah can travel through enemy territory by himself safely even with letters of safe passage. Pieces of paper will not be enough for those many different peoples who hate the Jews. So Neh. 2:9 tells us, "The king . . . also sent army officers and cavalry with [Nehemiah]."

This is one of my favorite verses in the story of Nehemiah. My reading of the circumstances is that Nehemiah, having lived in Persia all his life, really had no idea how difficult the journey would be. He believed that these enemies would let him pass by safely if he showed the king's letters to them. Later in the story, however, we will see how fiercely these enemies do not want this project to succeed and how they will directly attack it. They are not going to be tolerant of this attempt, even though Nehemiah will be appointed governor of the territory. In other words, Nehemiah is appointed by the king to be there and therefore operates under the king's authority. That is not going to be enough, however, to stop them.

King Artaxerxes has much more experience in these matters, and he knows of this bitter rivalry. So he protects Nehemiah by sending the army officers and cavalry with him. As we have been doing, we need to see the parallels for us. Nehemiah's journey home is symbolic of our journey when we want to return to our "home" in God. It is the journey of changing our lives in repentant ways so as to return to God's commandments. And the enemy, Satan, who has been against us since the beginning of time, in no way wants us to make that journey. He is going to attack us and seek to thwart us in any way he can. Satan also knows the places in our lives where we are the most vulnerable.

Knowing we will be attacked, what do we do? Where is the army, not to mention the cavalry? The answer is really very simple: the army can be found in those groups of men or women who are willing to stand with us against the attack.

I love movies and have since I was a small boy. I regularly think of which movies are my favorite ones. Clearly we all have to be careful about which ones we watch because the content of some of them is so sinful. Occasionally, however, in some movies there are scenes that really illustrate a point. One such movie for me is *Gladiator*. This is the story of a great Roman general, Maximus. In the opening of the movie he leads the Roman armies against the collected tribes of Germania and achieves a great victory, wiping out almost all of the Germans. In fact, as a German myself, I'm surprised there were any ancestors left for me to be descended from.

The emperor, Marcus Aurelius, loves Maximus so much that he is ready to pass on the control of power to him after he dies. He prefers Maximus over his son Commodus, who the emperor knows is not capable of real leadership. The son, however, has other ideas and kills his father and betrays Maximus, who has to escape. Eventually Maximus is captured and sold as a slave to a gladiatorial school in North Africa. There, given his skills as a soldier, he excels.

Eventually this school of gladiators is taken to Rome to participate in the re-creation of great Roman military victories in the city's famous amphitheater, the Colosseum. The gladiators will be the "actors" in these re-creations, and of course, many of them will be killed in the process. Maximus and many of his gladiator comrades are eventually led into the Colosseum in front of thousands of people. As they stand waiting, an announcer proclaims that re-creation for the day is going to be the second fall of Carthage.

In that battle, the great Roman general Scipio is going to do battle with the much-feared barbarian Hannibal. Hannibal, along with his barbarian horde, was historically one of the greatest early threats to Rome. In this re-creation "Scipio," with chariots borrowed from the "Egyptians," will surround "Hannibal" and annihilate him. Now the announcer points to the gladiators, including Maximus, and says, "I give you the barbarian horde." The gladiators are well aware they will be annihilated in this re-creation. Maximus, who knows how to command, takes charge as only great generals can do and says to the others, "Has anyone here been in the army?" Several of them say yes. So alluding to a tactic the army veterans would understand, he says, "We have a better chance of survival if we stay together."

When the chariots enter the Colosseum, Maximus says, "Come together." Instantly, the trained soldiers among them know to form the tortoise formation. This formation consists of Roman soldiers coming together in a circle and placing their shields together side to side and over their heads; it literally looks like a tortoise shell. Using this formation, Roman armies through the centuries were able to defeat other armies, sometimes against overwhelming odds. So there the majority of the gladiators stand, shields locked together. But some of the gladiators, not understanding this instruction or from overconfidence, stand outside the group and are killed instantly.

The men in formation, however, defeat all of the chariots. It is the protection of their shields, locked together, that brings them the protection they need to withstand the initial assault.

Rent the movie if you want to know the rest of the story, but understand, for now, the tremendous value of a group. Remember the parallels of these stories to our lives. We probably aren't going to be facing chariots any time soon, but we are facing Satan and his name is "legion." The apostle Peter puts it this way, "Be self-controlled and alert. Your enemy the devil prowls around like a roaring lion looking for someone to devour" (1 Pet. 5:8). Peter is perhaps also thinking of the Colosseum, because in his day Christians were being eaten by lions in that arena. Clearly Satan takes countless other forms and tells innumerable lies. Knowing all this, do you think for one second you are strong enough to withstand that by yourself? One of his lies might even be, "You don't need anybody else. You can do this on your own."

One of the most common accountability mistakes I see men or women make is when they say, "I have an accountability partner." That is well and good, but let me ask you, how often do you talk to this person and what do you say? Perhaps you talk to him or her once a week, right after church on Sunday. He or she says, "How's it going?" and you say, "I'm fine." Are you really fine? Maybe this whole interchange is right after you've done the behavior you've wanted to change. In fact, you're not fine; you're really shameful and discouraged, perhaps also sad. This is church, however, and you want to look good, so you lie.

Let's say it is Saturday night and you are tempted to do the behavior you're trying to change. You try to call your accountability partner. Too bad because he or she is not home and not answering the cell phone. Or maybe he or she is tired and doesn't really want to talk. Or maybe he or she says, "Oh, you'll be fine. I'll see you at church. Hang in there." Then—click—you're done.

⊛ POINT TO PONDER

I've never known anyone who has changed a negative behavior on his or her own or even with the help of one accountability partner.

⊛ QUESTION TO PONDER

- Have you ever tried to have one accountability partner?

- How long did that relationship last?

- Was it successful?

One of my clients, let's call him Bill, was trying to change the behavior of looking at Internet pornography. He had tried and tried by himself and had never been successful. Finally, he started to come to one of my groups for men. When I have a group, we pass out a list of all the men and all their email addresses and phone numbers. So Bill now has about fifteen phone numbers. He had a group of men, all of whom were committed to stopping this kind of behavior. Later in the week Bill was tempted to look at porn at 2:00 in the morning. He got out his list. He called the first six numbers on it and no one answered. It was the early morning. Then the seventh man on the list answered the phone. It seemed he was also up and also tempted in the same way. Together they talked until 5:00 in the morning, and neither one of them succumbed to the temptation. That is the way a group works.

Most people get the concept that groups are important, but many resist it for a variety of reasons. What they say is, "I don't like groups," or "I don't do well in group." I was like that too. For me, I think it goes back to my childhood when I didn't always feel I fit in that well on the playground or in the lunchroom. Many of us have those kinds of experiences. I also grew up in the church, and because I was always required to go to several groups, I got my fill of them early.

Perhaps the worst fear about groups is that we will be forced to reveal facts about ourselves that we do not want to reveal. We are afraid people will not like us if they really get to know us. Revealing ourselves also means we will have to talk about our feelings, and that is hard for most of us, as we discussed in the previous chapter. I can hear it now from the voices of so many of the people I work with, "I just don't like those touchy-feely groups."

The "feely" part is the fear that we will have to give someone a hug at the end of group.

Some people have the logistical concerns that they will not have the time for a group. Again, I hear voices: "I can't take the time away from job or family," or "Who will watch the kids?" or "That group meets a long way away (like the other side of town)." As you already know, I love many of the teachings and sayings of Alcoholics Anonymous. One of the sayings applies here: "We must be willing to go to any length to recover." For people in AA, stopping drinking is priority number one. That is because they know that if they don't stop drinking, they will lose everything else in their lives anyway. Another AA saying is, "Whatever you put in front of your recovery, you will lose."

✦ POINT TO PONDER

Getting started with groups is hard, and you will probably need to get over many objections.

✦ QUESTIONS TO PONDER

- Have you ever been part of a group?

- If so, what was that experience like?

- Have you ever been part of a group that was dedicated to changing a behavior?

- How was that different from other groups?

- What have been your objections to joining a group?

Accountability means you will need to participate in an army of support for yourself in order to resist the powers of evil that will attack and distract you from your purpose. Finally, I hear you saying, "Easy for you to say, but where do I find these groups?" Let me give you some practical suggestions:

- If the behavior you want to change is an addiction, there are an abundance of groups available. I've been mentioning much about Alcoholics Anonymous. It is not just for people addicted to alcohol. You can also go to AA meetings if you struggle with other kinds of drug addictions, although there may occasionally be an "old timers" meeting in which alcohol is the main and only thing. If you prefer attending meetings specifically for various drug problems, there are groups such as Narcotics Anonymous (NA).

- These days there are accountability meetings for so many different kinds of problems. There are twelve-step groups for sex addiction, food addiction, and gambling addiction. A recent search of mine found over one hundred "anonymous" groups in my area alone. I would suggest you simply google the behavior you want to change, and I'll bet you'll find a group for it. One of the more interesting groups I've ever been to is Emotions Anonymous, where you can find accountability for various mental health problems, such as depression or anxiety.

- I'm been gratified to see that within the last twenty years there have been a growing number of groups that are Christ-centered in their beliefs. As I said in the introduction, the twelve steps are completely compatible with Christian faith, but many of us prefer for the language used at groups to be biblical. One of the early groups that sought to apply twelve-step wisdom and create general groups for Christians suffering with different addictions is Overcomer's Outreach. They have church-based groups that are very general to all addictions. You are always advised to go to those meetings in addition to a specific twelve-step meeting for your addiction.

- In the last few years the greatest explosion of Christian groups for addiction and other mental health issues has been Celebrate Recovery (CR). This movement was started by Rick Warren, the pastor of Saddleback Church in Southern California. Celebrate Recovery groups meet one night a week and have a general time of worship and then break into smaller groups based on the problem you're dealing with. I think that CR is good, but it should probably not be used as the only group you go to, since their materials are very general and sometimes not specific enough to a particular problem.

- Many of us who specialize in a certain field because of our own problems have created biblically based workbooks that can be used by church-based groups. The ones I have written are for those struggling with sexual addiction. We partner with L.I.F.E. (Living in Freedom Everyday) Ministries. This organization has sought to start groups for sexual addiction in churches all over the country and throughout the world.

For other problems any list of specialized workbooks and materials I might try to provide in this short book would be hopelessly incomplete. Again, I would advise that you google phrases that include "Christian" and "groups" and your specific problem.

- And there are always groups for the spouses of addicts and others struggling with problems. The most famous, of course, is Al Anon, which is not just for spouses but for all those who live with an alcoholic. Al Anon is a very strong fellowship, and I have often advised spouses to go to Al Anon even if their husband's or wife's problem is not alcoholism but some other addiction. As for the primary addict or struggler, there are Christ-centered groups for family members. In our field, again, L.I.F.E. Ministries provides a wonderful workbook and creates church-based meetings for spouses.

- If you still just can't find a meeting in your area, there are three things you might do:

  1. Some meetings, such as Al Anon, can be attended by people with other kinds of problems, as I suggested earlier. In my early days of recovery from sex addiction I could not find any kind of meeting for that. So I went to AA meetings and I'm not an alcoholic. I still benefited from the fellowship and accountability of the group. When they asked me to tell my story, and they always do, I was honest with them about what I was really struggling with. It turned out that ten of the twenty men there were also struggling with sex. The next week those ten men and I started a group centered on sexual addiction. It was actually exactly what I needed, because those men had lots of recovery experience and were really able to help me.

2. These days there are many online meetings that you can find on the Internet. Our ministry Web site has links to some of the meetings for sex addiction. Meeting online is a stopgap until you can start or find an actual group. Face-to-face is always best. Remember point number one and remember that you may need to drive to a bigger town nearby to find what you need.

3. Finally, consult with your local pastor or therapist. He or she will usually know of men or women who are struggling with similar issues that you are. Suggest that you are willing to find materials to use if he or she would be able to connect you with those people and provide you with space either in the church or counseling center to meet. Many ministries, organizations, and twelve-step fellowships provide starter kits that will help you know how to set up and lead a group. In some cases a pastor or therapist might be willing to help lead the group.

You may run into places that have "support" groups and places that have "therapy" groups for your problem. A support group normally provides accountability that centers on the actual behaviors you are trying to change. You might have one member of the group who functions as your sponsor and is someone you will be in contact with every day. These groups are usually not led by one central person, but usually the leadership is shared according to the materials or workbooks being used. A therapy group is usually led by someone who is licensed or certified to do therapy. That might be a psychologist, someone who has a mental health license at a master's level, or a pastoral counselor (a pastor who has specific training in counseling). If you find a therapy group, be sure to always check out the leader's credentials and experience in handling your specific issue.

One of the ways to get started in accountability and find a group is to simply ask several people who know you to pray for you in your efforts. Then ask them to ask you frequently how your search is going. Tell them to pray unceasingly until you get connected and to not stop bugging you until you do.

⚙ POINT TO PONDER

You must be willing to go to any length, geographically, emotionally, and logistically to find the "army officers and cavalry."

⚙ QUESTIONS TO PONDER

- Have you been discouraged in the past trying to find people who can help you?

- Have you ever told anyone about that?

- Have you ever shared your struggles with family members or friends?

- If so, could they be used to help you find groups and serve as temporary accountability partners until you do?

- Do you need help with finding resources on the Internet because you're just not Internet savvy?

Finally, one of my most frequently asked questions is, "Can my spouse be a part of my accountability group?" The answer to that question is usually no. Chances are your spouse has been greatly hurt by the behavior you're trying to change and also has a lot of anxiety about how you're doing. To share with your spouse every detail of every temptation might be overwhelming. I do believe that all of us are accountable to our spouses for our behavior, but they shouldn't be the ones monitoring it. My wife and I teach about this dynamic often, and what she usually finds to be true with the spouses is that they don't want to be lied to and do want to be included in what is going on your life. I regularly check in with Debbie and let her know what I'm doing, where I am, if I'm going to be late, and so forth. Most importantly, I try to let her know what I'm feeling. Most of the time, I find that difficult emotions drive my temptations. The other day I was angry at a person who had said some unkind and untrue things about me. In the old days I would have let that feeling of anger fester. Anger is the chief emotion leading to the feeling of entitlement: "I deserve to act out because I need a break today." It was important for me to let Debbie know about that emotion. In doing so, trust is most easily maintained and I am not at all likely to act out.

I was once teaching a group of army officers at the U.S. Army College at Fort Leavenworth, Kansas. I showed them the scene from the movie *Gladiator* that I described earlier. After the lecture was over, a general came up to me and told me that Roman soldiers were not braver than their enemies. They were, he said, more disciplined. I asked him, as a general, what he commanded. He said that he was the leader of the Ninth Cavalry Division of the U.S. Army. As he said that, I thought of Neh. 2:9. We all need the "army officers and cavalry."

4

PRINCIPLE FOUR
ACCOUNTABILITY MEANS YOU MUST GET RID OF THE GARBAGE IN YOUR LIFE

With the army's help Nehemiah arrives at Jerusalem. Along the way he tells us that certain enemies are not happy he has come to "promote the welfare of the Israelites" (Neh. 2:10). One of them is a Samaritan, Sanballat the Horonite. At first he and his colleagues tease and ridicule Nehemiah, because they have no reason to believe he has any chance of success. Nehemiah reminds them that they have no historic right to Jerusalem (v. 20).

Nehemiah initially does not let anyone know what he is doing. He is most likely afraid his enemies will learn his plans. He, therefore, goes out at night to survey the damage to the city. I often think of how discouraging that must have been. Things were completely broken down. It is at this point, however, that Nehemiah begins to assert his leadership. After three days of this inspection he says to the people, "You see the trouble we are in: Jerusalem lies in ruins, and its gates have been burned with fire. Come, let us rebuild the wall of Jerusalem, and we will no longer be in disgrace" (v. 17). To which the people responded, "Let us start rebuilding" (v. 18).

Now the project was underway. I imagine that the enormity of it must have been overwhelming. Nehemiah, however, exercises wise leadership and divides up the work. Nehemiah 3 lists how that work is parceled out to various groups and families. Some got a certain gate, and others sections of the wall. Some worked very close to home and made repairs either next to or across from their houses (vv. 23, 28). Principle four of accountability is taken from my favorite verse in the chapter, verse 14, in which Nehemiah says, "The Dung Gate was repaired by Malkijah son of Recab, ruler of the district of Beth Hakkerem. He rebuilt it and put its doors and bolts and bars in place."

As you can imagine, Bible translators must have fun translating the Hebrew word *'ashpoth.* In the NIV the word used is "dung." The literal translation of the noun here is "ash heap" or a "dunghill."[7] Other translations have called it "refuse" (see NKJV). Whatever word we use, the Dung Gate was the gate from which all of the filth, garbage, trash, and raw sewage were taken. One might be tempted to think that Malkijah got the lowliest of the low assignments. He is the one whose job must have literally stunk. In reality, maybe the Dung Gate is, in fact, one of the most important gates in Jerusalem.

Have you ever been to a city that is having a sanitation strike and seen how garbage literally piles up? Have you seen the filth, smelled the stench, and perhaps observed the rats? What is often not seen are the diseases, viruses, and pestilence that are hiding and spreading. A city that doesn't get rid of the garbage runs the risk of an epidemic of diseases. Some would say that the sanitation system of any city or town is the greatest health benefit there.

Several years ago Debbie and I traveled to Mumbai, India, for a short teaching trip. When we got off the plane, we discovered that the airport sanitation workers were on strike. The whole airport was a complete dump, with trash all over and filthy water standing in the bathrooms (which after a long plane ride you definitely need to use). We were tempted to get back on the plane and demand to be taken home. Fortunately, we didn't, because we had a wonderful time with the Indian people.

I am sort of a history buff and some, like my wife, would say a bit boring with my knowledge of trivia. Undaunted, let me give you one of my favorite historical examples of the importance of sanitation. In the late nineteenth century the city of Chicago was dumping all of its waste into the Chicago River. At that time all of the waste was supposed to flow out to Lake Michigan, which it did, but often the tides and currents kept the waste close to shore. There disease festered, and a number of plagues infested the city. A brilliant civil engineer suggested that a canal be dug to connect the Chicago River to the Illinois River, which in turn flows into the Mississippi River and eventually out to the Gulf of Mexico. That is exactly what they did. A fifty-mile canal, the first of its kind, was dug to bring this about, and in so doing, Chicago was rid of the problem. Of course, some of us who have lived in southern Illinois could say that this is not the last time Chicago sent a problem downstate. But the story does illustrate how sanitation control can save the lives of thousands.

Dung gates are important. So what does that have to do with accountability? Simply this, for most of us to make changes in our lives through accountability, we are going to have to get rid of some of the garbage in our lives. Just as garbage dumps have different kinds of garbage, so we must look at the different kinds of garbage in our lives.

Paraphernalia Garbage

Let's first remember that you are trying to change a particular behavior. When you think about that behavior, ask yourself if there are any objects or materials that contribute to that behavior. Perhaps it is best to help you understand this by giving you examples.

- If you're a smoker and want to stop, do you have ashtrays, lighters, or (more basically) packs or boxes of cigarettes around your house or office? Any of this kind of "stuff" is a simple reminder of your habit. Take out the garbage!

- If you drink too much, the first thing a member of AA will do with you is help you get rid of all the alcohol you have around your house, in your office, or even in your car. Alcoholics Anonymous members are relentless and will do a thorough job.

- Did any of you see the scene from the movie *Fireproof*? The husband in that movie had a problem with Internet pornography, so one day when he feels convicted about it, he takes the whole computer out into the backyard and smashes it with a baseball bat. I'm not sure we always have to be that drastic, but if this is your problem, you may want to get rid of certain downloads or "stashes" of material. You may need to get rid of Internet access altogether for a while. Do whatever it takes to get the filth of the Internet out of your life.

- Maybe you eat too much and want to change that. Are there certain foods in your house you need to get rid of? Be relentless. When I became diabetic many years ago, I had to go through our house and get rid of any and all candy. Let me tell you, it was painful.

- Do you have a hard time getting rid of things? Some people are hoarders. A number of years ago my wife and I decided to get a Dumpster, a big one, and have it put in our driveway. Then systematically we went through our house asking ourselves why we were holding on to certain objects. We practically filled up that Dumpster, and then our neighbors came and asked us if we minded them putting some of their stuff in it. It was a really good community bonding experience.

Are you getting the idea? Some of you might be saying that the behavior you want to change is less obvious than cigarettes, food, alcohol, or pornography. You want to change being angry or impatient. You'd like to stop withdrawing and being too quiet. For this kind of problem, I would suggest that you look around your life and see if there are factors around that "trigger" you into that behavior. One main form of garbage to look for is your schedule. Is it so busy that you just don't have time for any relaxation? This makes you stressed, impatient, and angry. Is the garbage in your life all of the "junk" that you put into your schedule? Imagine the Dumpster. Are there appointments, tasks, clubs, organizations, duties, or obligations you need to get rid of?

◉ POINT TO PONDER

You need to get rid of actual physical junk or garbage that is polluting your life.

◉ ASSIGNMENT TO PONDER

Would you be willing to at least make a list of the things you need to get rid of? If you do, share it with somebody who will hold you accountable to do so.

Tom, again not his real name, was a pastor who got involved looking at Internet pornography. One of the church elders discovered him doing this at church. He was fired from his job, and his denomination began a healing process for him that involved counseling for himself and his wife, spiritual direction, and supervision from the head denominational official. After two years he did very well and had been completely free of problems with pornography. Tom was publically restored to ministry in a service that was very meaningful. All of this time he worked at an office supply store. After his restoration, he was hired at a new church, which required a move to another state. Tragically, I got a call from him two weeks into this new job and he told me the same thing had happened again, an elder found him looking at Internet pornography.

The obvious question was, "How did this happen after all of the hard work you did?" Tom told me that when he was packing up boxes for the move, he discovered in his basement a pornographic DVD he had hidden there years ago and forgotten all about it. Instead of throwing it into the garbage, he packed it, and when he got to his new home, he watched it again. That led him back into his old behavior and tragically to another dismissal from a very great church.

You see how important it is to get rid of all of the dung.

Ritual Garbage

All behavior has a backstory—a series of events and circumstances that lead up to it. In the field of addiction, we call this series of events a ritual. I am always surprised when someone tells me about doing a sinful behavior yet again: "I don't know how this happened. It just seemed to come out of the blue." This is sheer denial or, at least, a failure to understand reality.

All behaviors start with a thought about doing the behavior. The thought is usually triggered by some event, interaction, or stimulus. Perhaps it is a stressful event at work, an argument with a spouse, or a perceived rejection of some kind. We sometimes call these thoughts preoccupations, fantasies, or obsessions if we spend hours every day just thinking about the behavior. In the second book of this series I will be discussing how to prevent these kinds of thoughts from happening in the first place. For now, suffice it to say that a person can waste hours every day lost in preoccupations or fantasies.

Many great minds over the centuries have told us that what we put into our brains will lead to behavior eventually. One of my favorite thinkers about this was Michelangelo, who used to say that every work of art he produced was first conceived in his mind. Paul teaches us, "Finally, brothers, whatever is true, whatever is noble, whatever is right, whatever is pure, whatever is lovely, whatever is admirable—if anything is excellent or praiseworthy—think about such things" (Phil. 4:8). Such thinking will always lead to positive behavior. Likewise, negative or sinful thinking will lead to negative or sinful behavior.

Before sinful thoughts can lead to the actual sinful behaviors, there will need to be actions or preliminary behaviors first. In simplest terms an alcoholic must go to a bar or liquor store to get a supply of alcohol. Walking there or getting in the car to go there is part of the ritual. Those who overeat, likewise, must obtain food in one way or another. Those ways are their rituals. Those who watch too much TV will have their favorite shows, their favorite chair, and perhaps their favorite food to eat while they watch.

Gamblers may have secret bank accounts or credit cards they use to obtain the money they gamble with.

Rituals include the ways that time for the behavior is created. I was recently at the airport and cleared security and arrived at the gate. A young couple there was having an argument because the husband wanted to go back outside to smoke a cigarette, which would mean he would have to go through security all over again, and the wife feared they would be late for the plane. One of the men I was recently working with used to tell his wife he had to stay at work late because he had a deadline to meet. But actually he was having an affair and was really at the other woman's house. There are people who obsessively clean and organize. Buying their supplies, making lists, and avoiding all other activities are part of their ritual.

Rituals are as unique as people. Everyone is a little different. I have worked with hundreds of men who are addicted to looking at Internet pornography. While the common theme is the actual sin of looking at it, how they carve out time to watch it, where they put their computer, what time of day they sit down to do it, and how they hide their files of downloads may be completely different. For example, one of my recent clients simply waited until his wife was too tired and went to bed. That was his time to "act out." Waiting for her to go to bed was part of his ritual.

If you are getting the idea, you know that rituals are an important part of the cycle of the behavior you're trying to change. I and many others feel that if individuals allow themselves to get into their rituals, the negative behavior will quickly follow. So accountability will remind us that every behavior, object, excuse, or lie that is part of the ritual must also be stopped. Rituals may not be in themselves sinful, but they will lead to sin. Every person who wants to change a behavior will have to back up in time to figure out every step along the way that leads to doing the unwanted activity.

● POINT TO PONDER

You must be willing to do whatever it takes by stopping any and all rituals that lead to the behavior you're trying to change. Accountability will help you do that.

● QUESTIONS TO PONDER

- Many of us have had to keep a time sheet for work in which we account for every minute or hour of what we do. Would you be willing to do that for all thoughts and behaviors that lead up to your problem behavior?

- Would you be willing to ask someone else, who might be more practiced in doing this, to help you make this time sheet?

- Can you confront any roadblocks in your mind about how difficult it would be to stop this pattern?

- Do you feel that to do this kind of garbage removal, you will be following the same kind of discipline you did in junior high?

Thoughts That Are Garbage

In the twelve-step programs there are many colorful terms that get applied to the different behaviors group members say or do. When it comes to thoughts, I remember an early meeting I went to when my sponsor said to me, "Mark, that is just *stinking thinking.*" It was, in fact, accurate, and it was helpful to be reminded that my thinking was way off base. I find that in accountability I often have to check with others about the truth or validity of what I'm thinking. As we already know, garbage stinks and we need to get rid of it. This is really true when it comes to certain thoughts that pollute our brains. There are different types of "stinking thinking." Let me list several of them for you.

Delusions occur when we put thoughts in our minds that are just not true. They are not consistent with general objective reality and, more importantly, not consistent with God's reality. When we think something terrible is going to happen inconsistent with reality, it could mean we have paranoid delusions. If we think we are more important or powerful than we really are, we may be suffering with delusions of grandeur. One of the simplest forms of this is when we think that we can influence someone else more than we actually can or that we've hurt someone more than we really did. If we imagine certain scenarios in our mind we wish would come true, that is really a fantasy. We might fantasize about changing an outcome of something in the past, achieving some kind of success that would bring us lots of attention or affirmation, acquiring enough money so that we would be really happy, or finding our true love. When our fantasies are about true love, for example, we can certainly find enough TV shows, romance novels, or movies to support our fantasy. Any of these delusions may lead us into terrible behaviors. If we have a fantasy delusion about true love, for example, it might lead us into an affair.

Rationalizations are excuses. They are the reasons we tell ourselves why it is okay to do the behavior that we otherwise know is wrong. Rationalizations come in thousands of varieties. They occur whenever we explain why we did something wrong. We might say, "I was tired, confused, not thinking straight, or stressed out." One of the oldest rationalizations is, "Everyone else is doing it." In our current culture, for example, we know that almost 90 percent of Christian singles have had sex by the time they are twenty-nine. This is the group that has never been married. I'm sure that as all of them have looked around in our culture, they see what seems to be the fact—that everyone else is having sex.

But far and away, my personal favorite rationalization is what is called entitlement. I call it my McDonald's excuse because of the McDonald's slogan: "You deserve a break today." In one of my audiences I recently I had an executive from Burger King who asked me, "Couldn't it be your Burger King excuse—'Have it your way'?" The feeling of entitlement often happened to me when I thought I was working really hard. Since I have always been involved in Christian ministry, I would say to myself, "I've been working so hard for God that he won't mind if I take care of myself, even if it's a sinful way of doing it." I looked at lots of pornography, for example, with that excuse. I might also feel entitlement if things in life don't otherwise seem to be going my way. So I might say, "My wife is angry with me. What was I supposed to do?" I know a ton of Christian men who have excused (or justified) sexual sin because their wife said no to sex the night before.

Entitlement really means we are angry with something or someone. Much sinful behavior happens when we are mad at a spouse, a friend, and even God. I rationalized most of my sexual sin because I was angry with God for not taking away my lust, despite the fact that I had prayed and prayed that he would. I would say, "Okay, God, if you're not going to help me, then I'm going to go ahead and do this." I also behaved very badly when I was angry with my wife for something she said or something she did or didn't do.

All of these rationalizations mean I really need others in my accountability group to remind me how "crazy" I am for thinking in these ways. Has anyone ever said to you, "You're so full of garbage (or some other word for dung)"? This is a good sign that you need to get rid of that garbage.

Lies about ourselves and others are the core beliefs we believe to be true about our identity or someone else's. My good friend and colleague Pat Carnes was one of the first writers to talk about how these core beliefs lead to addictive behavior. Pat was the original one to write about sex addiction in his pioneering book *Out of the Shadows*. One of the most basic core beliefs he said most addicts feel is, "I am basically a bad, unworthy person."[8] In the broadest sense, this lie is called shame. Shame fuels a lot of sinful behavior. Mainly, we might believe that since we're such awful persons anyway, we should do what we want, because bad people do the kinds of behaviors we're about to do.

Shame has many tentacles. Another core belief built on the first can be, "If you knew me, you wouldn't like me." I am, after all, such a terrible person. This is the core belief that leads to lies. We think, "I can't tell you the truth because if you knew the real me, you would leave me." We all have anxiety about being alone, so we tell lies to keep people happy with us and in our lives. We can tell lies about who we are, about what we did or didn't do, or about someone or something else.

A third core belief is also built on the first: "No one will take care of my needs." Again, if I'm a bad person, then who would want to do anything for me? This core belief gives us a justification to do things for ourselves. Therefore, even sinful behavior can be rationalized by the idea that no one else is doing anything for me. No one cares, anyway, so why shouldn't we go ahead and do it?

Shame, as with any of these core beliefs, is often the result of messages from our families and others that we have heard or experienced growing up. Many of us did experience awful forms of abuse that convinced us we are bad. Some of us were neglected, with our basic needs for love and nurture going unfulfilled, so we come to believe that no one will care for us. All of these core beliefs are based on life experience, and they are lies. Many people, however, get so used to believing them that they really become lifelong victims. Have you ever talked to individuals and tried to convince them that God really loves them or that they are simply not as bad as they think they are? Have you felt as if you were talking to a brick wall because there were so many counterarguments? People get used to being victims, and they have a very hard time believing otherwise.

In the wonderful story about Jesus healing a man by the pool of Bethesda (John 5:1-9) he asks the paralyzed man, "Do you want to get well?" (v. 6). To which the man replies, "I have no one to help me into the pool when the water is stirred. While I am trying to get in, someone else goes down ahead of me" (v. 7). This man had a core belief after being paralyzed for thirty-eight years that no one had ever helped him and no one ever could or would.

To believe that we are so terrible and that no one will love us or help us is a garbage thought. It pollutes our very soul with despair. When we feel such despair, we are tempted to drink something, ingest something, eat something, or do something that will make us feel better. Many of the drinks, drugs, or foods we put in our system make us feel better for a while. One of my favorites, for example, is caffeine. Some of our behaviors can also create neurochemical reactions in the brain. Gamblers, for example, experience adrenaline because of the risk, fear, and excitement of winning or losing money. As one of the most power-ful drugs, adrenaline gives anyone a temporary feeling of relief from despair.

One of the greatest advantages of accountability is that our groups can remind us of what is really true, particularly in the sight of God. God loves us and has made us "fearfully and won-derfully" (Ps. 139:14). He has sent us his only Son to die for our sins. Shame is so much garbage in light of what God has done for us, and we need to get rid of it.

❋ POINT TO PONDER

Shame is a lie that binds us to despair and leads us into destruc-tive substances and behaviors to relieve it.

❋ QUESTIONS TO PONDER

- Which of the core beliefs that I've described are ones you've thought to be true about yourself?

- Can you recognize experiences of abuse or neglect in your past that led to these core beliefs?

- What reaction do you have if someone tries to remind you of the truth?

Our core beliefs of others are also formed by our life experiences. Like the core beliefs about ourselves, these act like a filter often causing us to misinterpret what others are doing or saying. Tony, for example, grew up with a father who often shamed him for not doing anything right. His mother stood by and did nothing to stop this. She was rather cold and distant. Today, when anyone gives him any kind of criticism, even constructive, he filters it through all of the shame messages from his past: "I'll never get it right, and they really don't like me." That is especially true in his relationship with his wife. When she is busy and not in a good mood, Tony filters that as a sign that she doesn't really love him. Core beliefs are powerful. Tony would often say to his wife, "Why are you so angry with me?" and his wife would be surprised he had experienced her words and actions in this way.

One of the early lessons I learned in accountability is that I, too, had many filters that often got in the way of my perceiving the truth. Often a filter would lead to anxiety, sadness, or anger on my part. Those feelings would cause me to react to others, especially my wife, in ways that would result in arguments. My accountability team, including my therapist, helped me to see that I was not always perceiving, that I was filtering, the truth. They encouraged me often to take a time-out, particularly in the middle of conflict or difficult reactions to people or life events. Sometimes just doing that, maybe taking a walk around the block, was enough to dislodge me from my core beliefs. At other times I would record what I was thinking in a journal and when I read back what I wrote, I could see how erroneous my thoughts were. Also it was always helpful for me while taking a time-out to make calls to my accountability group. Just hearing their voices was often enough to set me straight. There were times, also, when they would speak the truth to me and help me see the truth.

My general beliefs about so many things—men, women, work, God, church, roles, politics, and so on—were all formed in my youth and sometimes confirmed, in my mind, by my life experience. The work of getting the garbage out of my life consists of constantly asking myself the questions, "Where did I learn to think that way?" and "Do I still consider those beliefs or perceptions to be true today?"

I know for one thing that I came into marriage with many core beliefs about women and marriage. My wife also had beliefs about men and marriage. Together we have discovered that many of the beliefs we held are found in the book *Men Are from Mars, Women Are from Venus*. We now know that 95 percent of what we believed about the differences between men and women was all learned and not really true. Debbie is much better at math and money management than I am, and yet I came into marriage thinking all men were better at scientific matters and should lead their homes when it comes to money. We battled about that for years. How wonderful today it is to cooperate. Could it be that men and women are both from earth, not different planets, that God created us male and female, both in his own image? What a thought! Perhaps, with more similarities than differences we can be companions and not enemies. What a relief—I don't need to figure out life on Venus!

● POINT TO PONDER

Core beliefs about so many facets of life are formed in our early lives and are greatly influenced by the culture around us.

● QUESTIONS TO PONDER

- First, think about your mother and father (or the main person who raised you) and think of a story about each one of them that you now think has affected how you perceive yourself or others.

- That is a big assignment. Would you be willing to share these beliefs with someone else to check out how that person's beliefs about you or the world might be different?

- Can you think of an old belief you've had that you no longer have?

- Have you ever experienced or been aware that you misinterpreted something your spouse, a friend, or someone else was trying to tell you?

Pride Is Garbage

Members of Alcoholics Anonymous say, "My own best thinking is what got me here"—that is, "got me to an AA meeting because I'm an alcoholic." Paul puts it this way, "For the foolishness of God is wiser than man's wisdom, and the weakness of God is stronger than man's strength" (1 Cor. 1:25). Principle one of accountability stresses the absolute necessity of being humble and broken if we are going to change any behavior.

A while back I was meeting with a pastor who had been involved in an affair. He knew he needed to stop and never let it happen again. His wife had been forgiving. When I talked to him, however, he was full of his own wisdom, which he had gleaned from many sources including the Bible. I told him he needed other men in his life. He told me he only needed God. I said, yes, he needed God but he also needed others. He would smile and in that gentle pastoral tone assure me that he was "fine" and that he would get through this with God's help. Later he sent me a CD of a sermon series he preached on sexuality, fidelity, and purity. The phrase "the blind leading the blind" came to my mind. Later I learned that he had never discontinued the affair and that his church had finally asked him to resign. Arrogance and pride are terrible roadblocks to healing and change.

As a pastoral counselor I understand that biblically pride is really original sin. It is the inability to trust God and others. Having studied psychology I know there are many factors in our past that can make us distrustful of God and others. Putting that all together I know that arrogance is often a representation of our inability to trust and is the origin of such phrases as "false bravado." Arrogance and pride are hard to be around, and we want to tell people who have refused all offers of help and continually talk about their own strengths to shut up.

Pride is about pain, fear, anxiety, and sadness, and we need to try and understand how to help prideful people feel safe enough to ask for help. That is counterintuitive, I know. Prideful types don't seem to need any help. But they really do. Pride is garbage, and we need to get rid of it. Some of us will need to be patient and help them get to the "dump."

● POINT TO PONDER

Pride is the oldest form of garbage and has existed since the beginning of time. It gets us absolutely nowhere in bringing about change. We will need to find accountability to remind us to get rid of it.

● QUESTIONS TO PONDER

- What have you boasted about lately?

- Has anyone ever offered to help you and you have declined: "It's okay—I'm fine"?

- Make a list of the most humble people you know.

- Now ask yourself, as you know them, do these humble people ever ask for help?

Here is a final assignment for this chapter, and it's very basic. Make a list of garbage that needs to be taken out. Imagine a Dumpster arriving in your mind and ask yourself what you need to throw in it. Actually write down your list and put it somewhere you can see it every day. Share your list with at least one other person, and ask him or her to remind you about it and to ask you how you're doing about getting rid of the garbage listed on it. When you start this process, see if you don't feel lighter and even physically better. Part of what you'll throw out is all the stress this garbage creates. Getting rid of it is like cleaning house. You'll feel much freer. It will be like getting over an infection.

5
PRINCIPLE FIVE
PREPARE WHEN YOU ARE STRONG FOR A TIME WHEN YOU WILL BE WEAK

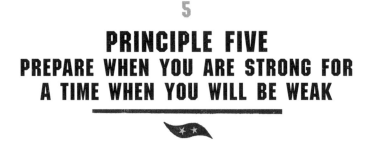

Now that the work of rebuilding the wall has been started, the enemies of the Jews get angry. First Sanballat (Neh. 4:1-2) and then Tobiah (v. 3) ridicule and taunt the builders, asking them, in essence, what they think they are doing. They are laughing at the work and mocking the builders. Tobiah's language is very colorful when he says, "If even a fox climbed up on it, he would break down their wall of stones!" These enemies know that the Jews have been unsuccessful in rebuilding for one hundred years. There is no historical reason for them to really think they will succeed.

As always, Nehemiah begins the response to this by praying. He asks to be heard by God, and then asks him to turn the enemies' "insults back on their own heads" (v. 4). He also asks God to remember the enemies' guilt (v. 5). Nehemiah then tells us that the work on the wall continued because "the people worked with all their heart" (v. 6). Since the ridicule does not produce the expected result, the enemies really get riled up and they plot to attack Jerusalem (v. 8). It is now getting much more serious.

This threat takes its toll. Nehemiah tells us that the enormity of the project begins to wear the people out (v. 10) and that the people were afraid, saying, "Wherever [we] turn, they will attack us" (v. 12). In verse 9 Nehemiah has already posted guards day and night to meet this threat, and now in verse 13, having determined what the weakest points of the wall are, he posts families at those places with all of their weapons.

The great strength of Nehemiah at this point is that he prepares. He knows the attack is coming, and he gets ready for it. He doesn't wait for the attack to come, he is constantly ready and anticipating it. Nehemiah knows that the enemy is capable and deadly and that everyone needs to be prepared. Simply stated, principle five of accountability is that we should prepare in a time of strength for a time when we know we will be weak and the enemy will attack.

One of the most common mistakes I hear people make about accountability sounds like this: "I know I need to make calls and go to group meetings, and I will when I get tempted." But this is much too late, because by the time we are tempted we may be way too weak to resist. In our story of Nehemiah remember that the enemy in the story is a representation of how Satan attacks. He is going to come after us at our weakest places. One of his lies is that we should go ahead and do the behavior we are trying to stop and not follow through with the behavior we are trying to start. At this point, our weakness is that of spirit—the feeling we really want to do it or, in the case of positive behaviors, we really don't. We are tired and vulnerable. We're not going to make calls or go to groups. Satan also attacks us by going after a weak place in our "wall," the place of selfishness. Another weak place is our tiredness. We say to ourselves, "We have been working long and hard. We are tired. We can let down our guard for a little while."

Another common mistake I often hear is this one: "I am being successful—the work is proceeding and I'm doing well. Don't you think God will reward my good behavior with the prevention of Satan's attack?" It's almost like saying, "I sure hope Satan will give up now that I have returned to God." In my experience, it doesn't work that way. As in Nehemiah's story, when we start to be successful, that is when Satan says, "I better really go after that person now to get him or her back."

The Bible is very clear about this principle. The word "guard" is used 126 times in Scripture. Perhaps the most succinct time is Paul's teaching in 1 Cor. 16:13: "Be on your guard; stand firm in the faith; be men of courage; be strong." This is exactly where account-ability comes in. Our "army" will need to remind us to be strong, have courage, and be on guard. Also remember that being on guard is never a matter of being alone. Nehemiah tells us that he stationed *families* at the weakest places of the wall (Neh. 4:13).

Figure Out Your Weak Places

The first step in preparing for the attack is to know where your weak places are. Where is it likely that you will be attacked? What is your Achilles' heel? Are you, however, one of those peo-ple who hates admitting you even have weaknesses? Perhaps one of the messages of your family was that you were always to be strong and that you were never to admit you even have problems. If this is the case, this is your first weakness, the message that you can't be weak. Ask one or more of your accountability partners to remind you of your commitment to "work the program" and at least read this section of the book.

I think weaknesses can be thought of in several categories:

1. **Ritual weaknesses.** One of the ways to start thinking about this is to remember, as you did in chapter 4, what your rituals are. What thoughts and behaviors lead you into your sinful acting out?

2. **Emotional weaknesses**. The places in your wall will be vulnerable when you are not strong emotionally. Alcoholics Anonymous has talked for years about HALT, which stands for hungry, angry, lonely, and tired. Even that is not a comprehensive list, although it is a good start. Hungry doesn't really refer to physical hunger (unless of course you are a food addict) but in this context means hungry, or even starved, for affection, love, affirmation, touch, relationship, and nurture. For example, you may simply need someone to say a kind word to you. Anger will often lead us into sin, because when we are so resentful of others, we think we deserve to do something for ourselves. Loneliness can often lead us into anything that symbolizes nurture to us, like food, sex, or inappropriate relationships. When we're tired, our defenses in general are way down. Let me add sadness, which can also be an emotion we seek to medicate by various substances and behaviors. Likewise, anxiety and fear seek to be "fixed," and we can turn to drugs, alcohol, food, sex, or work to take our minds off of worry. Finally, boredom is a weakness. Boredom demands we do something to find excitement, and some of the ways we might choose to do so, such as gambling, watching too

many TV shows, playing video games, or worse, may get us into trouble.

3. **Spiritual weaknesses.** Do you need convincing from me that if you don't take time for your relationship with God, you will be left very vulnerable to attack? Prayer, Bible study, and meditation are cornerstones of spiritual discipline. Remember again that accountability will be your army asking you if you're doing these things. Many of us, including myself, have been angry with God for not "delivering" us from our sins. We have prayed and prayed, and God, in our perception, has not answered. Anger at God leaves us rather rebellious against God, and our sense of sin diminishes. In accountability this anger is a very good thing to talk about with our brothers or sisters. As a good beginning, read some of the psalms or the whole book of Lamentations and see if it isn't true that only after expressing anger does faith return.

4. **Physical weaknesses.** I'm not talking about physical impairments or disabilities. Rather, these weaknesses are about not doing a good job of self-care. There are basic questions here such as, "Are you getting enough rest?" "Do you exercise?" and "Are you eating right?" Remember in HALT you will be more vulnerable if you are hungry, tired, or simply don't have enough energy. Included in this category of physical weakness are any mental health issues that are based on the health of your brain. Anxiety, depression, mood swings, and anger can all be affected by the health of your brain. You may find that therapy, support, eating right, and exercising help with these matters. For those of us in cold climates during the winter, not

getting enough sun might cause a form of depression. For some, talking to a medical doctor might mean that medication will return us to a better place. Ask your accountability partners to remind you about self-care, including the care of the most important organ of your body, your brain.

5. **ADHD as a weakness.** I recently read a newspaper report that said in the next five to ten years one in four adults will be diagnosed with ADHD, which means Attention Deficit Hyperactivity Disorder. This is a problem in the brain. People with ADHD have a hard time concentrating, planning ahead, and organizing their thoughts; they are impulsive or compulsive, and have difficulty supervising themselves and feeling empathy. Clearly people with this disorder have a hard time making healthy decisions. I have found that in the men I work with, roughly half of them have ADHD. Many studies have shown that adults who have ADHD will be twice as likely to develop an addiction if it is left untreated. In my experience there are times when people try to do all the right things to change their negative behaviors, but their brains are impairing their efforts. Ask your spouse, friends, and certainly your accountability partners if they believe you demonstrate the symptoms listed above. Then ask them to hold you accountable to getting an accurate diagnosis from a professional, such as a psychiatrist or psychologist. In this way you will be able to pursue the necessary treatment that may put you on the path to better decisions.

6. **Triggers as a weakness.** If you really want to know the weak places in your wall, you will need to know what triggers produce emotional reactions in your life. Triggers

could be any kind of stimulus that takes you to a place of sadness, anxiety, fear, or anger. When these feelings are triggered, it is more tempting to do something to get rid of them. People who smoke, for example, are often "medicating" anxiety and fear. Triggers are stimuli you may or may not recognize. If you have trouble overeating, going to the grocery store is an obvious trigger. But it may be less clear to you that watching someone else eat a doughnut might cause you to feel left out and prompt you to go out of your way and get a doughnut for yourself. Watching a sexually provocative commercial on TV might tempt you to find pornography on the Internet and eventually masturbate. That is obvious, but did you realize that when your spouse says no to sex, it triggers feelings of rejection in you and eventually entitles you to act out sexually in some way, perhaps by having an affair. Seeing the lottery numbers reported on TV or seeing the World Series of Poker on ESPN might trigger you to try your luck at the local casino.

Triggers are often related to past life events that were painful or hurtful in some way. Stacey, for example, was sexually abused by an older man when she was a girl. When she got married, looking forward the whole time to being sexual with her husband, she was painfully surprised to see how emotionally painful sex became. When her husband initiated sex, it was a trigger for her, returning her to her painful memories. She suffered with what we call sexual anorexia, a lack of desire for sex, until she got professional help with her trauma. Triggers like this very powerful one can cause emotional reactions that can lead us into many kinds of unhealthy behaviors. One of the challenges of triggers connected to past events is that the current event triggering the past emotion may seem of little importance, leading a person to think, "How could I have been so bothered by that really insignificant event? That was no big deal."

For accountability to work with this form of weakness, our partners will have to provide good ears for listening. Often our partners can help us sort out where the trigger came from and what it means. In severe cases, accountability will challenge us to seek professional help so that we can heal the damages of the past.

● POINT TO PONDER

If a person doesn't take his or her weaknesses seriously, these vulnerabilities will lead to great damage from the attacks of temptation.

● QUESTIONS TO PONDER

- Recall a time recently when you had an emotional reaction that seemed out of proportion to the event.

- When was the first time you remember a trigger like this happening? What story from your past is associated with this time?

- Has anyone ever asked you about whether or not you suffer with ADHD?

- Have you ever felt that your sadness, depression, anxiety, or anger was out of control?

- Has anyone ever suggested to you that you take better care of yourself?

- If you haven't already, make a list of the rituals that lead to your negative or sinful behavior.

Plan Ahead So That Accountability Happens Automatically and Not Accidentally

Now you are ready to plan. Every weakness requires a prevention plan. Every person is unique for what that plan needs to be, and there are some general components to think about.

1. **Phone calls.** Calling people is the cornerstone of most support groups. Most of us, however, don't like making calls very much. We say, "My cell phone weighs one hundred pounds." I have heard many people say over the years, "No one calls me." It is hard to make calls. Most of us haven't liked it since we were young. It is, therefore, a challenge that won't be easy for most. But it is vital. The main encouragement I can give you is that when you start making calls, eventually others will call you back. Think about getting in the habit of making at least one call every day even if you don't feel tempted that day. Perhaps nine times out of ten you won't need to make a call because of temptation. It will be the tenth day, however, that you will

need to make that call, and since you are in the habit of doing it, it will come more naturally.

I can also tell you that you will be surprised when one day you receive a call you didn't necessarily expect, and that call could make a difference in whether or not you remain pure, sober, or healthy. One man told me recently that simply listening to a voice mail was what stopped him from acting out.

The members of your "army" or support network are who you will call. In most support groups there is a definite expectation that you, too, will make calls. In my first support group, the man who "sponsored" me required me to make three calls a day, morning, noon, and night. One of those calls had to be to him and the rest to other members of the group. Carry a phone list of your accountability partners with you at all times. You might want to ask them to call you as a way of helping you get going.

2. **Meetings**. As I've already said, accountability depends on groups, and groups need to meet together regularly. It is at those meetings that you will always "check in" with how you're feeling and what temptations you might be facing. One of the regular activities of all groups will be helping you decide what's coming next and planning for it. In the early days of your change, temptations may be a daily (if not hourly) crisis. During these early times, you may even want to belong to different groups that meet on different days. Alcoholics Anonymous has a saying that you should go to "90 meetings in 90 days." Doing so is also a part of doing whatever it takes.

3. **Planning.** When you know all of your weak places, you will always need to have a detailed plan of how to avoid your vulnerabilities and temptations. Often this is simply a matter of establishing ongoing boundaries that clearly define behaviors you won't do. Alcoholics won't go into bars, food addicts don't shop by themselves or buy certain types of food, and gamblers will not carry any credit cards and no more than several dollars in their wallets. For me, there are many such boundaries that continue in place even though I have been sober or free of my acting-out behaviors for almost twenty-five years. I don't have private conversations with women at any time or in any place. I don't befriend women by email or on social networking sites. The only time I see a woman in my counseling practice is when her husband is with her or when my wife is with me.

All of these boundaries are constant. In the early days of my healing, my accountability group dramatically helped me know what these were. There were times when I felt I was back in junior high and needed a hall pass to go to the bathroom, but my group reminded me that all of the restrictions were part of my plan and my commitment to stay well. Today all of these boundaries are simply a natural part of my life that I rarely have to think about. And that is the point. Changes become habits, and habits are in place for those times when, if not for them being in place, temptation would overtake me.

There will also be times when planning involves special circumstances. You might need to have a special meeting or encounter outside of your normal boundaries. The holidays especially are times during the year when any of us might be around circumstances that involve unique temptations. And there are always those family gatherings that might be rife with triggers. Debbie and I always plan for holidays and have agreements in place of what we will do if temptations or triggers occur. We even go so far as to have code words that only we understand. In this way each of us will know what the other needs without anyone else even knowing what we're talking about. For me an early challenge was going on trips. Before I left for every trip, I made plans with my accountability group for how I was going to "head off at the pass" any possible temptations.

For example, a doctor I'm currently working with had problems with sexual encounters when he went on trips to medical training events. His wife, also a doctor, decided to forgive him and not leave him. So it was important to both of them that he plan for the next trip. He brought his need for that into our group. When he was done, he had an hour-by-hour plan for how he was going to avoid temptation on the road. It involved phone calls, visits with friends and family who lived in the city where he was going, emails to members of his group, and check-ins with his wife to let her know he was "safe." He returned without incident, and his group felt very proud of him for all the effort he had gone to.

● POINT TO PONDER

Staying healthy, sober, and pure will always involve "set in stone" boundaries and preparations for special circumstances.

✹ QUESTIONS TO PONDER

- How are you at making phone calls? Do you yet have a list of phone numbers?

- Would you be willing to make a call even if you don't think you needed to?

- List the days of the week on a piece of paper and indicate next to each day the meeting you will go to on that day.

- Make a list of all the ongoing/permanent boundaries you find necessary to keep in place in order to avoid temptation.

- What special circumstances are in the near future that cause you some alarm about your vulnerabilities and temptations?

- Are you willing to make a plan to avoid them?

Over the years of my work in the field of helping people change, I have seen hundreds of times that the people who are successful are those who know their weaknesses, accept them without becoming victims about it, and plan, plan, plan. They are the ones who are breaking the cycle of sin.

6

PRINCIPLE SIX
ACCOUNTABILITY MEANS BUILDING AND DEFENDING IN EQUAL MEASURES

Nehemiah is growing as a leader. When the building project started, his speech to the people was simple, but now that he knows the attack is coming, he gets more inspirational. He looks over his plans, and satisfied, he says, "Don't be afraid of them. Remember the Lord, who is great and awesome, and fight for your brothers, your sons and your daughters, your wives and your homes" (Neh. 4:14). This speech is a great reminder to us that our fight to change is not for our own selfish purposes. Rather, it is for those around us we love. It is in large part to serve them. The greatest motivation for my recovery was my desire to not hurt my wife again or pollute the lives of my children.

Principle five for the Jews is in place. The defenses are set particularly at the weakest places of the wall. Now principle six comes into play. Nehemiah says, "From that day on, half of my men did the work, while the other half were equipped with spears, shields, bows and armor. The officers posted themselves behind all the people of Judah who were building the wall. Those who carried materials did their work with one hand and held a weapon in the other, and each of the builders wore his sword at his side as he worked" (vv. 16-18). I love the image of those who carried materials having a sword in one hand and some kind of tool for building, such as a trowel, in the other.

Nehemiah had divided his workforce. Half built and half defended. It was fifty-fifty. Building and defending occurred in equal measures. Our biblical story is telling us that in accountability half of our time needs to be spent in defending against attack/temptation. The other half, just as important, needs to be spent building. As I have often done, my thoughts return to well-worn AA sayings. One of my favorites is, "If you're going to stop something, start something."

Let's begin by asking the question, "How creative were you in practicing the behavior you're trying to change?" I know people who have spent hours planning, preparing, and executing the behavior every day. Some do so to the point that other important activities, such as work responsibilities or family time, are sacrificed. For some of those behaviors, people have to be very creative to find time to do them and to make excuses about what they are doing. The lies told are often masterpieces of rhetoric.

I believe we are all built to be creative and productive. We long to build. God put creative energy in our brains so that we will "be fruitful and increase in number" (Gen. 1:28). I believe that our creative energy will not be denied. We might think we have no talents and can't create or build anything, but we all have some gifts and all have the ability to be productive. It is a force to be reckoned with. What happens, however, if this creative force is not used? It will always seek expression. Therefore, even in our most sinful of behaviors we are probably being creative and productive. Think, for example, of all the ways you might have created cover-ups for your behaviors.

For me, the worst times were when I had no deadlines and nothing at the moment to do. I was bored. It was then that I often found things to do, and some of them were not always healthy. I was talking to a man recently who told me that at his job he was expected to always be busy but that there were many times when his company just didn't have enough for him to do. Part of the problem was that he was so fast at what he did that he would finish ahead of others. His boss told him that whatever he did, he needed to look busy. So he invented things to do, and most of that involved the computer. One day, he had overheard a friend say something about how attractive some actress was and he decided to see if he could find pictures of her. One thing led to another, and before he knew it, he was looking at several movie scenes in which this particular actress had appeared nude. Now he was really curious and started thinking of all the actresses he had ever fantasized about, and through his computer investigative skills, he was able to find all of them in some sort of nude picture. More and more he used his work time to do his "investigations" until one day his boss talked to him about some things the IT department had found on his computer. He was creative, and the results of his "research" were productive, but it almost cost him his job.

If all this man did from this point on was to "defend" himself against computer pornography, he would eventually get tired and burned out. His challenge was not only to defend himself against "the attack" but also to figure out what he was going to do to be creative, to produce, to build something. So he installed filters and accountability software on his computer both at home and at work. The reports from his accountability software were sent to members of his group. He went to his meetings and made his phone calls. He was defending with one part of himself. Also he discovered he liked arranging pictures of his family into various online albums that he could send to them via the Internet. He used his computer skills to build some fun memories for his family.

Paul teaches us this in Romans, "For what I want to do I do not do, but what I hate I do" (7:15). Notice that he first says he doesn't do what he wants to do. Then he says, what he hates is what he does do. To me that means one of the best ways to stop something is to make sure all our time is spent starting and maintaining something else. Think about it—have you ever been so frustrated that you didn't do something positive, that you coped by doing something negative? There were many times when I was frustrated with myself for what I could not get done and I turned to an unhealthy behavior to make me feel better. How would you complete Paul's teaching, "For what I want to do _____ I do not do, but what I hate _____ I do."

What Are You Building?

Every project begins with an idea, and every idea leads to a picture of what will be built. Remember that Nehemiah had never been to Jerusalem and thus had never seen the wall or the city in its glory days. I believe, however, that he could see it in his mind. Every artist, every builder, and every writer has always begun with the picture of his or her finished project in his or her mind. As I write this book, the picture of the cover is in my mind. I can see it on the bookshelves. Are you getting the picture? When you finish this chapter, I want you to have a beginning vision of what you are going to build.

Physical Building

The concept of building can mean an actual physical building project. That can be very satisfying. One summer I remember thinking, "I need to replace one of the boards on my back deck." It was totally rotten. When I took out the one board, however, I found the one next to it was rotten also, then the next, and then the next. When I was done removing the boards that were rotten, there was no deck left! Then I had to build. Our whole family at some level participated. Our daughter is married to a civil engineer, so believe me—we had an exact picture of what that deck needed to be. The whole project was somewhat symbolic of this chapter. To change a behavior we may have to take out lots of rotten things and then rebuild from the ground up.

At other times in my life, I have always enjoyed building things. Pounding nails, painting, wiring, installing drywall, and plumbing have been nice distractions from what I normally do. At all times, I know that doing this with (in my case) other men has been very rewarding. One of my favorite times was when I invited members of one of my accountability groups to come over to my house and help me build a backyard shed. Is there something you've been wanting to build, large or small?

Remember that building is using your productivity and creativity. As such, it is channeling your energies away from negative behaviors and toward positive ones.

Character Building

One of the many gifts that working a twelve-step program gave me was the gift of knowing I needed to build a better character. In steps four and five of those twelve steps, I learned about all my moral character defects and that I needed to confess them. Then in steps six and seven I learned I must lean on God to "remove" those character defects. In short, I learned that I really needed to grow both spiritually and emotionally. I needed to build character.

That is no small task. When I started, I was facing some pretty severe consequences of my sin. It was a discouraging time. One of my first steps in building character was to remember that God was at work in my life, even in the hard times. The words of James came to me: "Consider it pure joy, my brothers, whenever you face trials of many kinds, because you know that the testing of your faith develops perseverance. Perseverance must finish its work so that you may be mature and complete, not lacking anything" (1:2-4). It is much easier to say now, but looking back I can see all the things God taught me about trusting him and how they helped me develop perseverance. I had lost a lot of things at that point in my life, but I clung to the idea that I was maturing away from sin and that even with the losses, I lacked nothing.

Over the years since then, I have seen my character building as I learned to stop blaming people for all my faults. I was the one who had made sinful decisions. Later in the same chapter James says, "When tempted, no one should say, 'God is tempting me.' For God cannot be tempted by evil, nor does he tempt anyone; but each one is tempted when, by his own evil desire, he is dragged away and enticed. Then, after desire has conceived, it gives birth to sin; and sin, when it is full-grown, gives birth to death" (vv. 13-15).

Over the last twenty-three years I have sought spiritual direction, counseling, groups, and accountability. All of it has developed character. I have had major defects of anger and anxiety. At each step along the way my group of men always reminded me of my need to work on those. My vision has always been to be the man God calls me to be.

What kind of character do you want to build? One of my favorite challenges is the one Paul set before the Philippians:

Rejoice in the Lord always. I will say it again: Rejoice! Let your gentleness be evident to all. The Lord is near. Do not be anxious about anything, but in everything, by prayer and petition, with thanksgiving, present your requests to God. And the peace of God, which transcends all understanding, will guard your hearts and your minds in Christ Jesus. Finally, brothers, whatever is true, whatever is noble, whatever is right, whatever is pure, whatever is lovely, whatever is admirable—if anything is excellent or praiseworthy—think about such things. (4:4-8)

If, with God's help, we all pulled off this instruction, what character we would have!

Relational Building

Perhaps your building project has a vision of building better relationships, such as with your spouse, your children, other family members, or your friends. Chances are good, as I know from experience, that depending on the nature of your sinful activity you have damaged some or all of your relationships. There are lots of workshops and seminars out in the world about how to better communicate, and one or several of those could be part of your building project. Going to counseling as a couple, as a family, or as two friends is also a possibility. Taking more time for the people with whom you want to build relationships is very important. There are so many practical things you might do. Although this is not a book on all the possibilities, here are several important relationship-building measures you might do, particularly if you have damaged a relationship:

1. **Confess your role in the damage,** own your responsibilities, and ask for forgiveness. This does not mean the other person(s) automatically will or even should reciprocate. You will feel better for doing so.

2. **Confession assumes you will disclose all the lies you have told and all the behaviors you might have done in secret** that betray your relationship. We find that sometimes with professional help, it is always beneficial to disclose your entire list of behaviors in a time line from start to finish. For example, when my wife and I work with a couple in which one of the spouses has sexually betrayed the other, we always ask the offending spouse to disclose all of his or her behaviors either from the beginning of the relationship to the present or from the beginning of the problem behavior to the present. By this I mean, for example, if one spouse has betrayed the other by looking at pornography, it is usually very helpful for that spouse to disclose when this problem first started and how it has progressed up to the present.

3. **Make amends to the people you have harmed** if you really want to have an ongoing relationship with them. Amends can take several forms. If you can repair damage in some way, do so. One of the easiest examples is that of having stolen money from someone. To pay that person back is obvious. Making amends for other forms of damage are not always so obvious, but you might ask the person what you could do. Another way of looking at amends is that you are promising to permanently change the behavior

that was damaging. Those who have sexually betrayed a spouse should be willing to be completely pure in the future.

4. **Seek to serve the other person.** Be a good listener. Affirm the person. Express your love to him or her and help that person to feel safe around you as best you can. You might even ask what it would take to help him or her with any and all anxieties he or she has with you. Learn how to be trustworthy. Tell the person you want to be his or her faithful spouse, parent, or friend for the rest of your life. Be honest and always tell the truth.

Some of these relationship-builders are not easy to do and may cause you to feel lots of anxiety. This, again, is where your accountability team comes into play. Ask them to help you "build" these actions and new healthy behaviors.

Building a Calling

Some people make the mistake of thinking that the word "calling" refers only to those who are called to religious service, either full or part time. While it is certainly true that pastors, missionaries, religious educators, and many other faith-based workers are called to their occupation, I believe all of us are called at some level to participate in God's plan for our lives. The word "vocation" is from the same root word as "voice" and, therefore, really refers to calling also. What can you build to participate in God's call on your life?

It has always seemed to me that God creates us "fearfully and wonderfully" (Ps. 139:14) and that part of that creation includes the gifts he gives us. In 1 Cor. 12 Paul teaches us about God's gifts to us and that they are of the same Spirit and given for God's purposes: "There are different kinds of gifts, but the same

Spirit. There are different kinds of service, but the same Lord. There are different kinds of working, but the same God works all of them in all men" (vv. 4-5). Have you ever considered that it is your "job" to build a calling based on these gifts? This does not mean you will always make money using them, because we are called to use them in various capacities.

How do you know what these gifts are? Before you think about this too long, answer one question: "What is it you are doing when you feel the greatest sense of passion?" You will know passion when you feel energized by doing this and not fatigued. You will know when you feel a sense of joy and fulfillment in doing it. You might know your passion when you experience others affirming you greatly for doing it. Perhaps you have been ignoring your passion for a lifetime. You might think that acting on it would be impractical and even impossible. You might think you are unqualified or ill trained. You see only the roadblocks. That is exactly where your accountability network comes in. Ask them what they think and what they have observed about you. One simple question is, "What have you seen me doing when you have observed that I do it with great joy, passion, or excitement?" Then ask them for encouragement to pursue it. Ask them to pray with you for God's guidance in that regard. Ask them for practical suggestions about what you need to pursue it. Get around people who are already doing it and ask them how they do it.

In my career today I consider that at least a part of my calling is to train and equip others to work in my field. I have been given the gift of teaching and that certainly fits with that calling. One of my favorite examples of how accountability principle six worked in my life occurred several years ago when I attended a conference where the main speaker was challenging the audience to take seriously the need to take the message of Christianity to Europe. He said, "How many of you here are descendants of Europeans? Your ancestors who came here from Europe brought Christianity to this nation. Today only 2 to 3 percent of Europeans go to church. Perhaps it is time to take your faith back to the country of your ancestry." I was moved to tears for some reason that I didn't immediately recognize, but I did think that such an emotional reaction meant something about what God might be trying to communicate to me. I said to myself that I am not trained as an evangelist or don't have that gift. Then I realized that my gift is teaching and that perhaps there was a need in one of the countries where my ancestors came from, Germany, for training in my field. Perhaps, I realized, one way to take a Christian message to Germany was to teach about the healing of an addiction that was alienating people from God.

Now the question was, "How do I build that calling?" So I decided to take the question to one of the men in my life who holds me accountable. Two weeks later both he and I were at a large Christian conference in one of the largest hotels in the world. There were eight thousand Christian counselors there, and we met for breakfast at one of the many restaurants in the hotel. I told my accountability partner that I felt called to go to Germany and teach about my field. I knew that this man had traveled extensively in Germany and that maybe he might know of a way to get me there. After he heard this, he asked me to get up and walk with him to the table right next to us. He greeted the person sitting there and said, "This is Mark Laaser and he is telling me he wants to go to Germany and teach." Then he said to me, "Mark, this is Dr. Ulrich Giesekus, and he is a German psychologist and also has a business doing Christian counseling seminars in Germany."

That is how God works, I believe. Share the vision of your calling with accountability partners and then step back because something is going to happen. Six months later, I was in Germany and "Ulie" had set up several seminars for me to teach to German psychologists, psychiatrists, and pastors.

Again, let me ask you, "What calling are you building?"

As I write to you now sitting here at my desk, I am aware I am building a book, word by word, sentence by sentence, paragraph by paragraph, page by page, and chapter by chapter. If I thought about the entirety of the project, it could be overwhelming, but tonight I have a goal of writing at least two pages. Gradually, the work of the "wall" is progressing. I am also defending myself against distractions. There are plenty of sports on the TV, but I'm recording them. There might be Internet sites to peruse, but I'm avoiding them. I notice I need a new "gadget" for my computer that could take me out to the electronics store, but I redirect my attention. Throughout it all, I remember I'm building and in equal measure defending against "attacks" of distraction. And I can tell you that doing this energizes me, and I know I'm in my "zone" of calling.

These are just a few ideas about what to build. My hope and prayer is that this chapter has started your own thinking about what you can build. Use your creativity, productivity, and passion, and you will find you hardly think about your old behaviors at all. As the old sports cliché says, "The best defense is often a good offence."

POINT TO PONDER

Building uses our creativity and productivity in a passionate and healthy way and "distracts" us from our old and unhealthy behaviors.

 QUESTIONS TO PONDER

- Think of something you have physically built that gave you a sense of accomplishment and fulfillment.

- What is one character quality you have always wished you had or were better at?

- What are the main relationships you would like to experience deeper intimacy with?

- Are there relationships you have hurt in which you need to confess and own your responsibility?

- If there are, what are your plans for amends?

- Think of some task, activity, career, or hobby you have dreamed about but didn't think you could do.

- Which of your accountability partners will you talk to about your answers to these questions?

I pray that you will find this chapter the most exciting and challenging one in this book. It is the work of building that will give you the greatest sense of energy.

7

PRINCIPLE SEVEN
TO CHANGE A NEGATIVE BEHAVIOR, YOU MUST DO WHATEVER IT TAKES FOR AS LONG AS IT TAKES

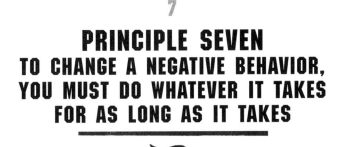

In Neh. 5, Nehemiah begins to describe to us how "taxing" the work of the wall was becoming. The people doing the work began to tell him how desperate they were:

> "We are mortgaging our fields, our vineyards and our homes to get grain during the famine." Still others were saying, "We have had to borrow money to pay the king's tax on our fields and vineyards. Although we are of the same flesh and blood as our countrymen and though our sons are as good as theirs, yet we have to subject our sons and daughters to slavery. Some of our daughters have already been enslaved, but we are powerless, because our fields and our vineyards belong to others." (Vv. 3-5)

In those days it was not an uncommon practice, as we see here, to even sell your own children into slavery. Times were really tough.

When Nehemiah hears and sees all of these things, he becomes angry because he knows that the rich who own the land are exacting fees and taxes on the workers. It seems that economic sociology hasn't changed that much over the centuries, since the rich get richer and the poor get poorer. Nehemiah calls this corruption "usury" (v. 7). As much as he can, he buys back those who have been sold, and then he confronts the usurers and tells them to give the money back (vv. 6-11). Would that we had such a champion today!

Needless to say, all of this was very anxiety producing to the people. They were trying to build and defend all the while worrying about how they were going to eat. Emotionally and physically they must have been exhausted. This is the way it often is for any of us who try to build and defend in order to stop old behaviors and start new ones. Our original adrenalin that gives us so much energy for the start of the project eventually wears off. Now we come to the mundane tasks. And the work can be expensive. This is when many of us face a new temptation that goes something like this, "All this work is too expensive and tiring, and I need to stop." Then we go back to our old behaviors just to cope with our exhaustion. The vicious cycle begins again.

It is true that to change an old behavior we may need to spend money. First of all, we need to recognize that we have probably spent great sums of money on our addictions and other sinful behaviors. Some of you may have even gone into debt doing so. Although we don't sell our own children into slavery today, how many of us have "mortgaged" the future of our spouse and children by the debt we're in? Debt can be so oppressive and depressing that we are just too emotionally exhausted to do anything about it. Again, we might turn to our old behaviors to cope with that.

While it is hard to admit, I know I have had to make an accountability commitment to clean up my financial behaviors. I have had the wonderful fortune of being married to a woman who has many financial skills. In our healing journey, we have worked together to turn our financial health around. There were days when we didn't know how we were going to pay for all the counseling and help we needed to get well. For example, when I was in treatment for my addiction, a part of the program was called Family Week. Debbie needed to be a part of that, and to do so she was going to need to travel three hundred miles to the treatment center. That involved paying for meals and lodging, not to mention the child care we needed for one week. It was going to be expensive. I had been fired from my job, and Debbie was working part time from our home. The shame of the whole experience, at that time, prevented us from asking our parents for help. So it was very tempting for her not to come. Where was Nehemiah!

We were both praying about this matter, and on the day when she made her decision about coming, a neighbor and Christian friend of ours showed up at the door and said, "I don't know what is going on and I don't need to know, but in my quiet time this morning I got the message that you and Mark are in some kind of financial distress and that you needed some money. Here is a check and please know that you don't need to ever repay it." The amount of the check was exactly what Debbie needed to come to Family Week. And that week is what saved our marriage.

Sometimes I am afraid to tell that story because it seems so unbelievable, but it is true, and to this day it is one indication that

God was with us. Nehemiah wasn't there, but God was. What I'm trying to teach you is quite simple. When it comes to change and healing, do whatever it takes, however much it costs, and God will find a way. Debbie and I counsel with hundreds of couples who are really struggling with an addiction or infidelity. We tell them they will need to go to counseling and workshops, read books, get educated, and do whatever it takes to get well. Many of them, in faith, are willing to do that. Some are not because the work is too tiring and expensive. Guess who are the ones who survive and thrive as they build a new marriage and who are the ones who don't?

Nehemiah sets a wonderful leadership example in our story by not taking the food allotted to him as the governor appointed by the king. Not only that, but his "staff" doesn't take the food either, and yet they all seem to have enough to eat (5:15-18). The biblical wisdom portrayed here is that when a person is not greedy or selfish, God does provide, a theme reiterated in many other parts of the Bible. How are you on the money anxiety scale and how centered have you been on money? In order to change, shouldn't we be willing to trust that God will provide?

My favorite story of this principle is the account of the rich young man who comes to Jesus and asks him, "What good thing must I do to get eternal life?" (Matt. 19:16). In their conversation Jesus tells him he should obey the commandments, which the man says he has done. Then Jesus says he should sell what he has, "give to the poor," and follow Jesus, and then he will have eternal life, or "treasure in heaven" (v. 21). However, the man becomes sad and walks away because his wealth is great (v. 22). Jesus then tells his disciples, "I tell you the truth, it is hard for a rich man to enter the kingdom of heaven" (v. 23). I don't really think Jesus is telling all of us to not have wealth, but I do think he is teaching us about our attitude toward money. The key to the story is that Jesus wants this young man to follow him. Any person must be willing to do that whatever the cost. And when we do follow Jesus, we will change.

Do I need to tell you again who you will need to remind you of these truths? Yes, of course, they are your accountability partners.

⊛ POINT TO PONDER

You will need to spend whatever it takes to get the healing necessary to change.

⊛ QUESTIONS TO PONDER

- How much money have you spent on your addiction or unhealthy behavior?

- Are you in debt?

- How much do you think it will cost to participate in the resources you will need to heal and change?

- Would you be willing to discuss a plan for all of this with your accountability team?

In Neh. 6:1, Nehemiah tells us the wall is almost completed. There are no gaps left and only the doors need to be set in place. All military attacks have failed, and when the enemies, Sanballat, Tobiah, and Geshem, learn about the near completion of the wall, they know they must find another way to defeat the project. So they send Nehemiah a message four times, inviting him to a meeting in some house "on the plain of Ono" (v. 2), which is a long way from Jerusalem. This might be the first time that rival parties in this region of the world have been invited to a peace talk. Since the conflict there is as old as patriarchal times in Israel, I'm not sure any peace talks in that region will ever be successful. Clearly, the goal of these "peace talks" is to get Nehemiah to come down from the wall, to distract him from the work, and to kill him.

As we think about the relevance of this for us, my experience in helping men change reminds me that for them, as it was for me, the most dangerous time of the healing journey comes when we think it is almost complete. I have seen it over and over again. People feel confident that their work is almost done. They are satisfied with themselves, and they are tired of the work. Perhaps they are tired also of a label, such as addict, that has been given to them. Then, I believe, the enemy sends a message: "You are so tired, and you've been working so hard. You deserve a break. It's time to relax. After all, you've got this problem licked. Don't you hate being called a problem? Come out and play. Don't be so serious." It is all so tempting. Remember, too, that the messenger can come in all kinds of forms. Today I have seen an epidemic of problems that have been created by people getting together because of this message: "Would you be my friend on Facebook?" It might be someone new, old, or even an old girlfriend or boyfriend. Next thing, a meeting on the Plain of Ono, aka Starbucks, has been arranged and an affair begins.

Perhaps anger at all the work, labels, and inconveniences creates a sense of rebellion. So you venture outside the wall and get "killed" by your old problems again. If you are ever at this point, remember what Nehemiah says to the enemies: "I am carrying on a great project and cannot go down" (v. 3). I love Nehemiah's simplicity. It is not a complicated decision he ponders over. It is clear—the work is too important and he's staying on task. Remember that for yourself and have your accountability group remind you. Your work is important, so don't let the enemy distract you.

And just when you think you've withstood that temptation, the enemy is not done. Now Sanballat sends his aide with a personal, unsealed message in which he says there are rumors. The rumors are that the Jews are planning to revolt and that Nehemiah is trying to be king. Sanballat's message is that Nehemiah better come down and talk before these rumors get back to the king (vv. 6-7). Does any of this sound familiar? It should, because these kinds of malicious rumors are how the Jewish leaders in his day got Jesus crucified. The report to King Herod and to the Roman governor was that Jesus wanted to revolt and that he wanted to be their king. In fact, that is what a lot of the people wanted. Why else would they have chosen a revolutionary, Barabbas, over Jesus when Pilate gave them the choice (see Matt. 27:16-20)?

Nehemiah is a man of persistence, fortitude, and simplicity. He says, "Nothing like what you are saying is happening; you are just making it up out of your head" (Neh. 6:8).

What does this mean for us? For me, over the years the comparisons have been many. It is not that anyone has ever said I have tried to be king, but there have been those who have said I was trying to be too well known or important or influential. There have been those who have circulated false rumors of other kinds.

One former colleague of mine, who was jealous of my success, accused me of having an affair with another colleague. All of it was not true but for some who heard it, like those at a large national ministry, the damage is still something I'm trying to overcome. You don't know how many times the words of Nehemiah come to me: "You are just making it up out of your head."

One of the problems you may face in your journey is the same kind of jealousy about your success. While there will be many in your accountability group who will support and encourage you, there will be others outside your support system who just don't get it and really liked the old you. Believe it or not, there are those who like the status quo, even when the status quo is unhealthy. My now deceased younger brother, who was himself a pastor, never took care of himself. He lived according to some of the same ways everyone in my family had learned to cope. Much of that coping was normal, but parts of it were unhealthy. I remember when I came out of treatment and he knew I had changed, he said to me, "Mark, when can we be a normal family again?" The answer to that is, "Hopefully, never." In other words, "I'm not coming down from the work on the wall." You see, he died and I'm alive. While his death grieves me still, sometimes it's that simple.

What will this dynamic be like for you? There will be those old friends and family members who will want you to be the "same old you." This despite the fact that they know the same old you was not really happy and content. They might even be in as much denial as you were that the same old you is negative and destructive. Some might accuse you of being arrogant, uppity, or self-righteous. You might in fact be a little "preachy" about how good you're doing. There is nothing quite like a recovering addict to preach the virtues of sobriety to those who still suffer with addiction. There will be some who might resist the good things you're doing simply because they don't like to see you succeeding. It reminds them of how bad they're doing, and so they rebel against any of the good advice you may have. When you encounter this, remember the simple words of Nehemiah: "I am carrying on a great project and cannot go down" (v. 3).

The enemy is still not done. There is one last attempt to get Nehemiah away from the work. He visits the home of a shut-in named Shemaiah, who invites him to go with him to the temple. The reason is, he says, because there are men coming to kill Nehemiah. In other words, it is dangerous out there, come to the temple and be safe (v. 10). Nehemiah realizes that Shemaiah has been hired by his enemies, who want to discredit him by showing he is a coward. Again, Nehemiah is very direct and very simple, "Should a man like me run away? Or should one like me go into the temple to save his life?" (v. 11).

The truth of the situation is that the work is very dangerous. Nehemiah is not the type of leader to remain in safety while others take the risks. He is an "out front" type of man. He leads by example. Notice how continually wise Nehemiah is to discern the true intentions of others. I like to think that since he had been in the court of King Artaxerxes for many years, he was wise to the ways of political intrigue. He knew a deceitful plot because he could read between the lines of all the messages. Remember, being the cup bearer to the king, he was well aware that there were those who might want to harm the king. He had seen it all and, as such, was exactly the perfect man for this job.

For us, who seek to change and heal, often the work will seem very dangerous too. It will feel at times that we must take a certain amount of risk to do the new behaviors we have been told will heal us. For one thing, when we learn how to start telling the truth to others, we will confront the anxiety that gets us to think, "If they really knew me, they would hate me and leave me." This is really true for spouses who must tell their husbands or wives the truth about their old unhealthy behaviors. They have been lying about it for years, and now they must "come clean." Debbie and I often help couples through a time of "disclosure" in which (in our work) a husband confesses and outlines all of his sinful sexual behavior. I can tell you that when couples come into the room for that session, they are scared. With support, and with courage, they get through it. We have usually found that this truth telling, this risk, forms the foundation of a more intimate marriage.

Maybe for you it will mean having the courage to go to a new group, like one of the twelve-step groups. Perhaps it will mean confessing your sins to your pastor. For some it might mean facing very difficult decisions about life circumstances. Many of the men I work with find it is really hard for them to change their unhealthy behaviors because of the travel their jobs require. I have often been amazed at how courageous they have been to resign and find a job, perhaps for less money, because it provides them with more time at home and more safety.

Debbie and I were invited to speak at a large church in Seoul. As the date for our trip got closer, the North Koreans started experimenting with nuclear capabilities and made it known to the world. There were countless people who said to us, "Maybe this is not the right time to go to Korea. It is very dangerous there right now." There were even some who said, "You go, but why are you taking Debbie?" One of my friends who was a pilot of a 747 jet and often made the flight to Korea said, "Mark, do you know what happens if you overshoot the runway at the new Inchon Airport—you wind up in North Korea." "Funny," I said. The day of our trip arrived and we sat at a fast-food place in the Minneapolis airport. I was greatly anxious that we were being irresponsible. I remember that Debbie took my hands and said, "If God wants us on this trip, he will protect us." It was pretty direct and simple. At that moment, in my weakness, Debbie was my Nehemiah: "The work is too important, we're not coming down" (v. 3, author's paraphrase). Needless to say, we weren't blown up and had a very meaningful trip.

Have you noticed as you've read this book and considered the changes you need to make, what anxieties have arisen for you? What are your fears? You see, even as you read, the enemy is capable of sending you a message: "You really don't want to do this. It is too dangerous."

● POINT TO PONDER

Accountability will mean your accountability partners will often need to remind you that the enemy sends false messages and plots and schemes to get you away from the work. Accountability reminds you to stay on the wall.

● QUESTIONS TO PONDER

- Have you tried to change before and found you became tired of all the work, restrictions, and labels?

- Has that tiredness led you to let down your guard?

- How have your family and friends been with your plans to change or your beginning accomplishments? Have any of them invited you back to the "old ways"?

- What are the major fears and anxieties you have about change? Make a list of them.

There is a consistent theme in both Neh. 5 and 6. Nehemiah is willing to do whatever it takes for as long as it takes. Undoubtedly he is tired and frightened, but at every temptation, every problem that arises, and every distraction he stays focused on the task. He stays up on the wall. Finally, we learn that the work on the wall is completed in fifty-two days. I imagine that was not nearly as long as most people thought it would take. That is not always the case with big projects. They usually take longer. This summer our city began a renovation project of our street. It included tearing it up, putting in new water and sewer lines, and replacing the curbs several feet wider than they had been. Of course, that meant some of our beautiful boulevard trees had to be cut down, our driveways torn up, our mailboxes removed, and our yards cut into. In short, it was a mess. Continually the city promised us when they would be done, but the work went on past the promised completion dates. Finally, this fall, at least a month late and after the first snowfall of the season, all of it was accomplished. I think along the way at least one member of the construction crew was fired and replaced. Would that Nehemiah had been the project manager!

It is tempting for us to think at some point the work is done. I have talked to countless men who think that after thirty days of sobriety or change they have accomplished and finished the work. If you will read on, however, in the book of Nehemiah, you will see, starting in Neh. 7, that although the wall is finished, the work inside the city is just beginning. There are houses to be rebuilt and families to be restored to them. As always, I love the analogy. You see, when we rebuild the wall of defenses around us, the real inside work is only just beginning.

I wonder how "displaced" your family has been because of your behaviors. How has your "house" been destroyed? What will that work of restoration be like? Clearly we are not building an actual wall around ourselves. The work of change, healing, what we call "recovery," is actually about building healthy boundaries so that the enemy will have a much harder time attacking us. The early work of accountability uses the seven principles to establish those boundaries and thereby to maintain safety. Those boundaries are the beginning. I love a quote from Winston Churchill after the Battle of Britain during World War II. He was speaking about the accomplishment of winning the initial air war and establishing some safety from German planes for the British people. He said, "This is not the end. It is not even the beginning of the end. But it is, perhaps, the end of the beginning."[9]

That is what your initial application of the seven principles is also about. It is the end of the beginning. Now you face the life-long interior work you must do. That will affect your family and all your relationships. You will rebuild your house, and your legacy will be great. So know that the first time you practice the seven principles, you will find how challenging they are. As you apply them continually in your life to all things, not just negative behaviors you want to change, you will find they become a normal part of your life.

Alcoholics Anonymous members know that they are "only one drink away" from being back in their darkness. If you have ever had the chance to talk to one of them, he or she would gladly tell you that "working the program" is a way of life and a joy. They could not imagine giving up the accountability path they have learned. So will it be for you. I predict that in several years the principles you have learned here will be so much a part of your life, you will begin to wonder what life was like without them.

☀ POINT TO PONDER

We are never done until God calls us home.

☀ QUESTION TO PONDER

- Are you willing to do whatever it takes, however much it costs, in spite of your fears, for as long as it takes?

CONCLUSION—
ACCOUNTABILITY IS A LIFESTYLE

But if a wicked man turns away from all the sins he has committed and keeps all my decrees and does what is just and right, he will surely live; he will not die. None of the offenses he has committed will be remembered against him. Because of the righteous things he has done, he will live. Do I take any pleasure in the death of the wicked? declares the Sovereign LORD. Rather, am I not pleased when they turn from their ways and live?
—Ezek. 18:21-23

I am often asked by my clients, "When do I get to stop being an addict? When can I be normal again?" These questions have translations. Really what is being said is, "I'm tired of the label, and I'm tired of all the work. I'd like to be normal again." It doesn't always help to tell them that the old normal, or status quo as we've just learned, is killing them. What does help is to tell them that what they are being asked to do is really what I would ask any man or woman to do. In our current culture with all of its messages of immorality, every one of us needs to be on guard. Against the ways of the world, we all need to have a vision of God's calling in our lives so that our minds can be transformed. I tell them that by practicing the seven principles of accountability, they are way ahead of most people.

That is what I intend for everyone I work with—a new normal, a new status quo. In this new normal, being accountable is so much a part of life that eventually you won't have to think about it as consciously as you did at first. Accountability becomes a lifestyle. As a diabetic, I remember all of the things I needed to learn about healthy eating. I needed to count calories, understand the different kinds of sugars, and count the carbohydrates in everything that went into my mouth. I had to weigh my food and eat at regular times. I was supposed to exercise every day. Most difficult for me, at first, were all the times during the day when I had to test my blood sugar. And my dietician and doctor wanted me to keep a daily journal of the food I ate and the blood sugar results I got. I remember thinking, "I don't have time for this!" But today much of this is so much easier than it was then. Back then I remember feeling very different and alone. Plus I had a whole bunch of doctors and dieticians regularly holding me accountable.

A funny thing happened in our culture as people gradually accepted healthy nutrition as a vital part of our health. Many people are now counting carbs, fats, and calories. All of the foods that have been healthy for a diabetic are strangely enough now healthy for everyone. Exercise is also much more widely accepted as a vital part of everyone's routine. The main thing is that today I don't feel so alone in all of this. There are plenty of people, diabetic and nondiabetic, who share my lifestyle choices.

In my case, the necessities of my management program, which at first seemed so severe, eventually became normal, a regular part of my lifestyle. It's not that I don't think about all the things I do. Early on a friend reminded me of a scripture passage that to this day I say to myself whenever I am tempted to get discouraged about what I need to do. Paul tells us,

But we have this treasure in jars of clay to show that this all-surpassing power is from God and not from us. We are hard pressed on every side, but not crushed; perplexed, but not in despair; persecuted, but not abandoned; struck down, but not destroyed. We always carry around in our body the death of Jesus, so that the life of Jesus may also be revealed in our body. For we who are alive are always being given over to death for Jesus' sake, so that his life may be revealed in our mortal body. So then, death is at work in us, but life is at work in you. (2 Cor. 4:7-12)

For me being diabetic is simply a reminder that my spirit is more important than my physical body. Likewise, working an accountability program for diabetes reminds me to be account-able in all other areas of my life as well. Even though I have been sober for twenty-three years from my primary addiction, I never take my recovery for granted.

I hope this book will be helpful to you in the days ahead. Most of all, I want you to know that whatever behavior or be-haviors you are trying to change, you can succeed with the help of others. If you will follow the seven principles I've presented, and if you are patient through the process of change, you will be amazed at how much better your life becomes. Then, I hope, you will become a "missionary" for accountability to others. Don't be an arrogant preacher. Tell your own story of how you changed, and you will always find a brother or sister.

Most of all, I pray that God will bless you in all of your ef-forts.

NOTES

1. See "Bill's Story," chap. 1 in *The Big Book Online*, Alcoholics Anonymous World Services, http://www.aa.org/bigbookonline/en_bigbook_chapt1.pdf (accessed May 11, 2011). See also *Wikipedia*, s.v. "Bill W.," http://en.wikipedia.org/wiki/Bill_W (accessed May 11, 2011).

2. "Step Four" in *Twelve Steps and Twelve Traditions*, p. 42, Alcoholics Anonymous World Services, http://www.aa.org/twelveandtwelve/en_pdfs/en_step4.pdf (accessed May 19, 2011).

3. "Step Five" in *Twelve Steps and Twelve Traditions*, p. 55, Alcoholics Anonymous World Services, http://www.aa.org/twelveandtwelve/en_pdfs/en_step5.pdf (accessed May 19, 2011).

4. Mark Laaser and Debbie Laaser, *The Seven Desires of the Heart* (Grand Rapids: Zondervan, 2009).

5. See John Gray, *Men Are from Mars, Women Are from Venus* (New York: HarperCollins, 1992).

6. "Researcher Links Weekly Church Attendance to Longer, Healthier Life," University of California, http://www.universityofcalifornia.edu/news/article/4132 (accessed July 8, 2011).

7. *Blue Letter Bible*, s.v. "'ashpoth," http://www.blueletterbible.org/lang/lexicon/lexicon.cfm?Strongs=H830&t=KJV (accessed May 19, 2011).

8. Patrick Carnes, *Out of the Shadows: Understanding Sexual Addiction,* 3rd ed. (Center City, Minn.: Hazelden, 2001), 171.

9. Winston Churchill, "The End of the Beginning," speech at Lord Mayor's Luncheon, Mansion House, London, November 10, 1942, Churchill Society, http://www.churchill-society-london.org.uk/EndoBegn.html (accessed July 8, 2011).

RESOURCES

One of the dynamics I have observed over the years is how often contact information, Web sites, and the availability of books change. We are living in an electronic age and so much of what we read is on the Internet. So rather than list books or articles that I find helpful, I encourage you to stay in touch with the most recent material by regularly checking Web sites or doing Internet searches for information relevant to your needs.

There are two Web sites that will most likely continue to be current:

1. Our Web site is www.faithfulandtrueministries.com. On it you will find articles, videos, references to helpful books, and other counseling resources. A calendar of our workshops and speaking engagements throughout the country are included as well. We also provide, without charge, general education to the public through Web-based seminars, or Webinars. We will likewise be offering training Webinars for professionals, such as pastors and counselors, with the possibility, in some cases, of participants earning CEUs. Lectures by Debbie, other colleagues, and myself will also be archived on this site. Material from this book series will at times be presented as well.

2. Another Web site is www.aacc.net. This is the site of the American Association of Christian Counseling. The AACC is the largest association of Christian counselors in the world. This site has a directory of counselors in your area.

You will also find on this site several video training series on a number of topics. It is possible to get trained as a lay counselor or certified in several areas as a professional counselor by using these video courses. Some of those video series include Debbie and me. The AACC also conducts large national and international conferences that are a joy to attend. It is the best place to network with colleagues and friends. So stay in touch with what they are doing.

When lost in the maze of the Web, please call or email us directly. I, Debbie, or one of our staff will get back to you with specific questions. We enjoy pointing people in the right direction.

Mark R. Laaser, MDiv, PhD
Debbie Laaser, MA
Faithful and True Ministries, Inc.
15798 Venture Lane
Eden Prairie, MN 55344
952-746-3880
mlaaser@faithfulandtrueministries.com
dlaaser@faithfulandtrueministries.com
www.faithfulandtrueministries.com